Yarn Spinning Handbook

A Hand Spinning Guide for Spinners to Learn How to Spin the Wheel or Spindle with Wool Fiber to Create Yarn Designs Plus Tools, and Supplies Included

By

Zera Meyer

Disclaimer

This publication is designed to provide competent and reliable information regarding the subject matter covered. However, the views expressed in this publication are those of the author alone, and should not be taken as expert instruction or professional advice. The reader is responsible for his or her own actions.

The author hereby disclaims any responsibility or liability whatsoever that is incurred from the use or application of the contents of this publication by the

1

purchaser or reader. The purchaser or reader is hereby responsible for his or her own actions.

Table of Contents

Introduction

Yarn spinning is the technique of utilizing a spindle or spinning wheel to transform plant or animal fibers into yarn.

For almost 10,000 years, people have spun fibers into yarn or thread. While the first yarns were twisted rather than spun and were manufactured without equipment, most spinning was done using a spindle for millennia. The thread is made on a drop spindle as the spindle spins while gravity draws it to the ground; on a suspended spindle, the spindle is spun on a fixed surface, like a top, and the thread is formed by pulling the fiber away from the spindle. In the late Middle Ages, the spinning wheel was brought to Europe.

The introduction of the spinning jenny in the mid-eighteenth century mechanized spinning, kicking off the Industrial Revolution.

Spinning is broken into two parts: fleece preparation and spinning. Before the fibers are ready to spin, they must be cleaned, washed, and carded. While complete fleeces are still easily available and inexpensive, many spinners nowadays spin from rovings (cleaned and carded fibers that have been drawn out and slightly twisted to form lengths suitable for spinning).

Today, hand spinning is now primarily done for personal use, such as knitting, embroidery, or crocheting (very few people weave with their own yarn).

This book, *Yarn Spinning Handbook*, aims to equip you with the knowledge of how yarn spinning works and educate you on the processes of turning animal fibers (specifically, wool roving) into yarn vis-à-vis the tools and supplies required to get started. You will also learn how to ply yarns for different projects, common problems associated with yarn plying and yarn spinning, in general, are also covered in this book, and so much more!

So, without further ado, let's get the ball rolling.

Chapter 1

Yarn Spinning Fundamentals

What is Spinning?

In crafts, spinning is the method by which yarn is made from fibers. It is often used to refer to the handcraft used in yarn production, but the production of yarn with machines works in a similar way. Spinning yarn involves many unique steps; often, it includes the preparation of the fibers and then plying several yarns together. Yarn can be made from several kinds of fibers, and to work with them, you'll need to employ different procedures. Machine spinning is likewise a difficult procedure, despite the fact that this sort of yarn production is not traditionally seen as a craft.

Various tools can be used for hand spinning. It is also feasible for yarn to be made with no tools, although this is so hard and, most times, inaccurate. The drop spindle is the least tool for producing yarn, with yarns being made by twisting fibers using a weighted stick. It is still regularly used to produce yarns by hand and can create attractive yarns of a high standard.

Spinning wheels, on the other hand, are a sort of tool used to make yarn. They spin at a quicker rate when compared to drop spindles, but not as quickly as the industrial spinning machines. Using a wheel to produce yarns requires special abilities, but it is significantly faster than when you work with a spindle. Spinning wheel designs comes in various forms, each of which works in a somewhat different way. Considering the importance of yarn in the manufacturing of fabrics, numerous high-efficiency machines have been developed by various groups.

Sheep's wool is commonly utilized to make yarn. Nonetheless, different fibers suited for spinning are obtainable, and each produces a different type of yarn.

Animal fibers from sheep, alpacas, and other fur-bearing animals are widely utilized in producing yarn. Plant fibers can be spun into yarn, though some are mostly used more than others. Synthetic fibers are getting more common, and they can be utilized to produce yarns with a wide range of qualities based on the material.

Spinners routinely work with fibers at different phases of yarn production, making yarn production a fascinating activity. The spinner could dye, spin, and utilize the yarn, but they may also be active in the fiber harvesting process. For example, those with a small-sized herd of sheep are active in all stages of yarn production, resulting in a highly personalized result. A spinner can spin yarn for a particular project if they partake in each phase of the process. Though machine-made yarns can be incredibly consistent and appealing, handmade yarns have a long history that is appealing as well.

The History and Evolution of Spinning

Hand spinning is a centuries-old technique of twisting fibers together to produce yarn for garment making and other items. Hands were used to spin yarn for thousands of years using simple tools. The spinning wheel was introduced in the middle ages, making spinning yarns much easier. Presently, some individuals still spin yarn and other fibers with their hands. Continue reading to learn about the historical evolution of hand spinning and how it differs from industrial spinning.

History

Spinning fibers together to produce yarn has been practiced for more than ten thousand years. Decades ago, hand spinning was done out of necessity and not during one's leisure time. In the old days, slaves were the individuals that performed this textile work in making fabric that made up the garments and bed linen for the elite and powerful. To make these strands of yarn, workers utilized spindles and looms to carry out this tedious job. Some have argued that spinning fibers was a skilled occupation. Still, the historians believe this line of work or profession was unskilled labor that was meant for the poor and ignorant, generally a place for women of the lower class. However, this thought process has changed over the years.

Hand Spinning vs. Industrial Spinning

Spinning was done by hand and out of necessity, according to history. Almost every home in society took part in this laborious work. In the homes, machines and tools were put up to prepare for the spinning days.

Everything involved in the spinning process, from rearing the animals for sheering to growing cotton and silk crops, was more like a family activity in which everyone was involved. The task was difficult, arduous, and tiresome as members of the family assisted in manufacturing cloth from scratch. This was the only method available for making blankets before the industrial spinning machine was invented, thereby making the spinning task much simpler for families. Industrial spinning consumed less time. Factories started making fabric materials quicker than what could be made at home (homespun), making their product cheaper. However, those who maintained their home spinning craft were known for quality workmanship.

Materials

If you want to perform hand-spinning as a hobby and produce those beautiful handmade pieces of material to put on display while showing off your handy work, you will need a few supplies for success in this craft. A drop spindle and some wool or silk are required to get started. However, other materials can be used in hand-spinning: cotton, alpaca, angora, and mohair fibers. You will have to note that at the early stages of spinning, you have to decide where you will get your wool or cotton, being ready to shear a sheep as the need arises. Also, keep in mind when weaving fibers together, there are three stages before getting to the finished product. The three stages are handpicking, hand carding, and the spinning form.

Spinners utilized drop spindles and suspended spindles in the early days, with each spindle having its own method of pulling the threads or fibers in the process of spinning. The spinning wheel is another machine also used in making yarns; however, it was not in existence until the late Middle Ages, making its debut in Europe. Before the Middle Ages, the drop spindle was the most popular spinning machine.

Modern Day Hand Spinning

Spinning has progressed since the days when drop spindles were the only way to spin. Spinners in modern culture and spinning art have a wide variety of spinning wheels to choose from. Spinning wheels are accessible for both novices and those with greater experience in spinning techniques; for example, you can switch from a Saxony Wheel (used by newbies) to a Great Wheel (used by expert spinners) once you've mastered the art of spinning.

Benefits of Hand Spun Yarns

Let's take a look at some of the benefits of hand spinning.

Low Cost

If you create your own spindle, it will be less expensive. But buying a first-class spindle is also relatively cheap and will last longer.

You can get spinning fibers either for free (from the sheep farmer next door, your neighbor's long-haired dog, or your daughter's long-haired rabbit) or for less (and one pound of wool will last a long time). If you purchase luxury fibers like cashmere, the yarn you spin from them will still be less expensive than buying the yarn.

Provides Total Control

When you switch from sheep to sweater, you control every step of the way. Some people say they are allergic to wool (if it is a true allergy and not just a normal reaction to scratchy wool). It may be allergies to some substances used in treating the wool between shearing and the finished ball of yarn, e.g., detergents. You can work without these substances if you begin with raw fleece.

But if you purchase ready-to-spin fiber (that has been washed more aggressively than you would at home), you still have total control over the yarn you produce. If your sweater comes out too soft and "pilly," spin the yarn for the second one much tighter. You are responsible for the choices and consequences. Which are not disastrous - most times, the yarn can be used for something else if it turns out awful.

Hand Spun Yarn is a Tactile Dream

Knitting has a meditative effect to it, and the feel of wool flowing around and through a person's fingers and needles is one of the most enjoyable aspects of the craft. Hand spun yarn is ideal for knitters who enjoy the experience of knitting. The feel of hand spun yarns is one of the things that differentiates them. It has a lot of life in it. Mill spun yarns lose some of their inherent shine and bounce because they are firmly bound on cones, skeined, and packed in boxes for delivery.

Hand spinners can create yarns using a range of techniques to enable every breed of sheep's wool to pop through while assuring high quality because of the care necessary for spinning, setting, and preserving each skein of yarn.

Can Make Your Projects Pop

Handspun yarn is unique in appearance. Hand spun yarn offers a unique aesthetic that yarns spun commercially cannot match, whether it is the subtle variations in a fractal 2 ply, the beautiful stripes and round form in a Navajo 3 ply, the diversity and feel of a thin and thick, or an evenly spun natural colored fleece. Mild irregularities in yarn weight lend a particular handmade feel to the project you're working on and contribute to the feelings you're getting from it.

Ability to Work With Specific Breed of Fibers

Working with various lovely and distinct sheep wool breeds can help take your knitting to another level. Most hand spun yarns are breed-specific; they are not a combination of different fibers. A particular sheep breed births them. Using various breed-specific fibers can help you have a deeper insight into the factors that make a yarn the best fit for a particular project. Choose Shetland or Romney wool if you want a hardy, cozy, rustic yarn. Blue Faced Leicester is a smooth yarn that will give your knitted project a beautiful drape. Cashmere, Cormo, or Angora are all excellent choices for a baby project. The style of your knitting objects increases when you have a sound knowledge of your fibers and use them properly.

Hand Spun Yarn can Feature Creative Blends and Textures

Good yarns for decorations and weaving in knitting projects are art and textured handspun yarns. Most of the time, creative blends and textures are unavailable in commercial yarns. You can create texture by using nylon, bamboo, and silk as add-ins; for effect, you can add feathers. This makes your project unique.

Problems With Spinning Your Own Yarn

You can get addicted to spinning and lose interest in other activities. It might cost you more than you initially planned on completing your collection of hand spindles, as you might be attracted to more beautiful designs. Also, with a collection of spinning wheels in your living room, you must be careful while moving around.

Health problems can also result from spinning. Due to the repetitive movements used for one style of spinning, repetitive strain injuries (RSI) may result. Tendinitis can also affect the thumbs due to spinning; problems with

Achilles tendons might also result. So, to avoid health issues, watch your posture, be very relaxed as possible and take breaks regularly, mainly at the beginning. Altering your spinning (long-draw, short-draw, right-handed, left-handed) is also helpful.

Chapter 2

Yarn Spinning Terms and Definitions

Alpaca – a camelid family animal that produces alpaca, the luxury fiber.

Angora rabbit – the rabbit with long hair that produces angora, the luxurious fiber/wool.

Batts – carded hunks of fiber gotten from a drum carder.

Bench – also referred to as a table. The wheel and spinning machinery is set on a table spinning wheel.

BFL – Blue Faced Leicester wool gotten from sheep.

Bobbin – this is the spool shaft onto which the spun yarn is wound on a spinning wheel.

Carders (or cards) are brushes used to smooth and straighten fibers in preparation for spinning.

Comb – used in processing long stapled wool for worsted spinning.

Crimp – the number of curl available in a lock of fleece; fine wool is quite crimpy.

Distaff – a staff holding the flax or wool fibers that are taken from the flax or wool as needed by the spinner. A distaff can be joined to a belt, placed on a spinning wheel bench, or stand-alone.

Draft – the elimination of fibers so that just a certain amount of fiber can be twisted into thread.

Drafting triangle – the space between the spun yarn and the fibers that are being pulled out.

Drive band – the cord that coveys power from the big wheel to the pulley/ bobbin or spindle.

Drop spindle (hand spindle) – a stick having a whirl with weights used for twisting fibers into thread.

Ewe – a female sheep that is mature.

Fiber – the hair/wool/plant material not spun (unlike the thread, which is spun already).

Fleece – the complete wool's coat sheared off a sheep.

Flyer – the u-shaped mechanism twisting the yarn on a treadle spinning wheel.

Footman – is the long piece of straight wood or wire that creates a connection between the treadle and the spinning wheel's axle/crank.

Grease wool (or "wool in the grease") – the wool which comes off of a sheep that has not been washed.

Hank – a skein of wool 560-yard long, mainly wound around a niddy-noddy or reel.

Knot – a 40-yard yarn of strand skein wound around a reel or niddy-noddy that measures a circumference of 2 yards = 80 yards.

Maidens (or sisters) – two straight pieces of wood that hold the spinning mechanism horizontally.

Mother-of-all – the spinning wheel's whole spinning mechanism: flyer, maidens, and bobbin.

Navajo ply – a technique in plying that chains a single thread into a yarn with three-ply.

Niddy-noddy – a tool with double-heads used to skein yarns that have been spun.

Noils – short fibers discarded during fleece combing; can be blended with other wool and carded and spun.

Orifice – the eye or opening of the spindle present on a spinning wheel's treadle.

Pencil roving – tiny roving strips approximately the diameter of a pencil.

Plying – the process of twisting yarns together (two or more) in the reverse direction from which the yarns were spun.

Rolag – a finger-sized carded wool roll set to be spun into woolen yarn.

Roving – carded wool of long tubes, made by carding machines.

S-twist –This is a spun yarn having a counterclockwise twist.

Scour – the process of washing or cleaning fibers or spun yarns.

Skeining – the process of winding yarn from the spindle.

Skirted fleece – grease wool whose dirty edges all around it have been removed.

Sliver – strips of batts in a continuous strip.

Slub – the fat area in the yarn (sometimes spun in intentionally for novelty yarns) Note: fiber's staple cannot be shorter than the slub length.

Spindle pulley – the small grooved whorl containing the drive band linking the spindle with the drive wheel.

Staple – the length of a single strand or a lock of fleece.

Strick – a collection of flax, arranged for spinning after removing the tow (only long fibers).

Tops – long fibers made straight by combing.

Tow – the short fibers remaining after combing the flax.

Treadle – a mechanism that pushes the main wheel pedal, or the foot pedal thereby moving the main wheel.

Whorl – the spinning-supporting weighted part of a drop spindle. A spinning wheel spindle's speed is also controlled by the spindle pulley.

Woolen – yarns produced from short-stapled wool; that felts well and with a soft finish.

Worsted – created from long-stapled wool that has been combed longitudinally along with the fibers and spun from terminal end to tip in an apparel-style fashion; has a good finish and normally does not felt (i.e., jacket material, most tweeds, or suit)

Z-twist – spun yarn having a clockwise twist.

Draw – in the spinning process, draw is a technique for pulling fibers out. Long and short draws are used in this method.

Leader – to begin spinning new yarn, a piece of yarn is fastened to the shaft of a bobbin called a leader.

Spinning count – a measurement of wool diameter and is defined as the number of yarn hanks that can be spun from one pound of clean wool top

Skirting – is the process of removing unwanted wool, second cuts, stains, and vegetable matter from the fleece of wool before it is processed or sold.

Chapter 3

Getting Started With Yarn Spinning

Tools and Supplies

Let's take a look at the tools and supplies needed to start spinning.

What You Need to Get Started

Hand Spindle

A spindle is an upright spike made usually from wood and used to spin and twist fibers such as wool, flax, hemp, cotton into yarn. Weights such as disc or spherical objects called whorl are usually attached to either the bottom, middle, or top of the spindle; however, several spindles are not weighted by a whorl but by thickening their shape towards the bottom.

Spindles are available in various weights, but I recommend starting with one that weighs roughly 2-3 ounces.

Modern hand spindles can be classified into two:

- Drop spindles

- Supported spindles

Drop spindles are mainly available in high whorl (top whorl), low whorl (bottom whorl), and center whorl (middle whorl) versions. In a high whorl spindle, the whorl sits close to the top of the shaft so that the spindle spins very fast. To secure the emerging yarn in place, a hook is inserted over the top of the shaft, and the freshly spun yarn is wound around the shaft underneath the whorl in a cone form called cop.

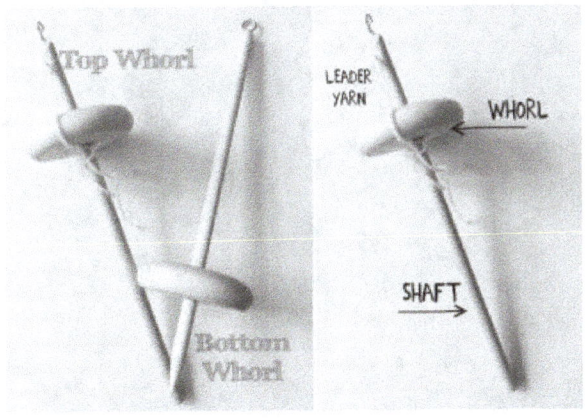

In a low whorl (bottom whorl) spindle, the whorl sits close to the base of the shaft, which allows it to spin slower, but more steadily and longer. The most recently spun yarn is wound around the shaft just above the whorl. The cop is mainly built on top of the whorl in center whorl spindles.

Most supported spindles spin with the tip on the spinner's thigh, on the floor, in a tiny bowl, or on a table. The size and shape of these spindles vary widely depending on the type of fiber and yarn they were designed to spin. A woolen-style yarn is frequently made with supported spindles. Fibers are spun with a long pull, either supported, unsupported, or both, and the spindle can be controlled with one hand. They're ideal for spinning short-staple fibers like cotton, yak, camel, and cashmere.

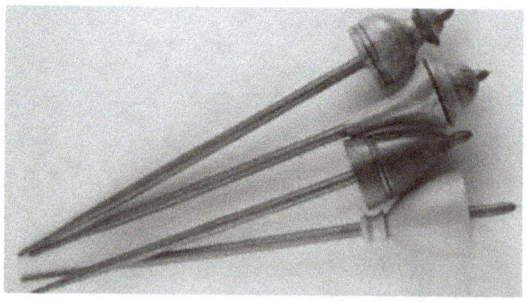

Spinning Wheel

The majority of spinning wheel models, except some specialty wheels, will help you master how to spin quickly and produce a lot of mid-weight yarns. That aside, important differences exist and with just a little planning, you can give yourself a head-start. Some factors to take into consideration at the outset and some questions that could provide you with guidance are listed below:

- Do you have limited or large space?

- Do you want to take your wheel along with you to groups for spinning or for travel?

- Do you find yourself attracted by traditional looks or prefer something that's modern?

- Do you want to spin mainly mid-weight yarns, or will you focus on super bulky or fine yarn?

As we discuss selecting a spinning wheel, we will consider some parts that make up a spinning wheel. These parts are similar in function among several other wheels:

SPINNING WHEEL PARTS

BOBBIN PULLEY/WHORL
FLYER
ORIFICE
MAIDENS
MOTHER OF ALL
FIBER BEING SPUN
DRIVE BAND
DRIVE WHEEL
TREADLE

Now, let's make some comparisons. With some knowledge discussed subsequently, you can get a wheel that looks right, feels right, and spins beautiful yarns.

First Comparison: Traditional vs. Modern Wheels

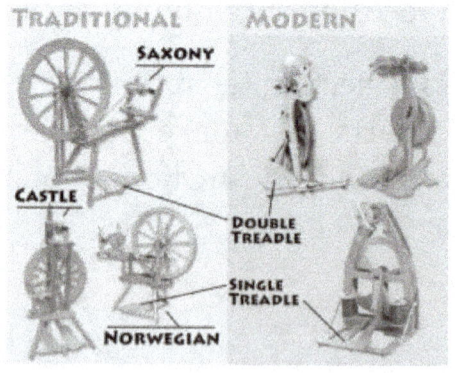

TRADITIONAL   MODERN

SAXONY

CASTLE

DOUBLE TREADLE

SINGLE TREADLE

NORWEGIAN

Traditional Spinning wheels:

- These are the ones found in storybooks. Rumpelstiltskin used the Saxony spinning wheel.

- Usually, it has ornate construction and may consume more space than modern wheels.

- Unable to be folded for travel.

- They still make use of modern parts. Also, they are versatile, spins well enough and quickly.

Modern Spinning wheels:

- There are lots of modern spinning wheels, with various shapes and sizes

- Focus mainly on function than traditional design.

- They can be folded, lighter, and have a little "footprint."

- Evolves faster to add new ideas, trends and improvements.

The Verdict: Which Design is Perfect for You?

Spinning wheels operate in similar ways, and they share similar parts, irrespective of the design (traditional or modern). If you like the traditional look, have a good space to accommodate a large wheel, and won't move around with your wheel, you should go for the traditional design.

On the other hand, if you prefer a lightweight wheel that you can easily fold and move around with, has versatility, and incorporates new trends, then a modern spinning wheel is your best bet.

If you don't have a solid preference, you should keep an open mind because other criteria could assist you in narrowing your choice.

Second Comparison: Single vs. Double Treadle

Treadling is the process of spinning the drive wheel by applying pressure on one or two treadles below the wheel. A single or double treadle might appear like a huge decision, but most often than not, it is more of what your preference is.

Why Choose Double Treadle:

- Treadling with two feet gives some rhythm that you would like

- Double treadle might be easier for beginners to control

31

- The work is divided between both feet, providing more opportunity for control and division of the work

- You can treadle with one foot if you prefer it

Why Choose Single Treadle:

- They can provide you with an elegant and more traditional appearance

- Its parts are fewer with less complex design and maintenance

- Switching of feet is easier, and you can relax one leg while the other works

- Changing orientation toward the wheel is easier.

The Verdict: Double vs. Single Treadle

A double treadle is better for beginners than a single treadle because it is less complex in controlling speed. Nonetheless, the difference is minimal and with some practice, learning to use a single treadle won't be an issue. The equal motion of double treadle might be better, especially if you have troubles on your back or other health circumstances, and you would gain from an always-balanced treadling motion. However, for many individuals, these differences are not "deal-breakers."

Single treadle spinning wheels are good for those whose preference is more traditional and with a simple design. They are also good if you prefer some extra freedom on how you familiarize yourself with the wheel.

Several wheels come with both treadling styles, so go for double treadle but don't rule out the opportunity to use a single treadle, even if you are learning.

Spinning Wheel Drive Options: Scotch, Irish, Double Drive, etc.

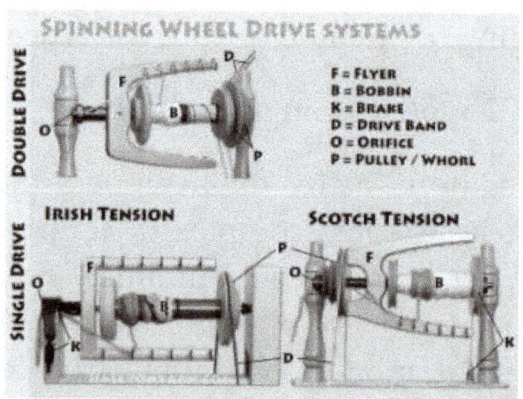

When searching for a spinning wheel, it's common for people to talk about single drive "Scotch or Irish tension" and "double drive" wheels. You can even be asked about your preference. Don't feel perplexed; these are just the several ways you can control the amount of twist added to your yarn and how fast it is wound onto the bobbin. You can learn the art of spinning on any tension system. Let's take a look at some similarities and differences:

Similarities:

- Fiber leaves your hand, passing via the orifice to the flyer: the spinning of the flyer adds twist to make yarn

- The bobbin preserves the twisted fiber/yarn

- Both the flyer and bobbin spin: if both spin with similar speed, then only twist is added, and the fiber would not be wound onto the bobbin

- Pulling back on the spun fiber adds "tension" by slowing the yarn from being wound onto the bobbin, which adds more twists. When tension is released, yarn is wound onto the bobbin.

Differences:

- Scotch tension: the drive band spins the flyer; it spins always. Pulling on the fiber makes the bobbin spin with the flyer to add an extra twist: otherwise, the bobbin brake slows it to wind on yarn.

- Irish tension: the drive band turns the bobbin: it spins always. Pulling on the fiber makes the flyer spin to add an extra twist; if not, the flyer's brake slows it to wind on yarn.

- Double drive: Both the bobbin and the flyer are driven by a driving band; the bobbin quickly spins, but more twists can be added when it slips.

Drive Options: The Verdict

Single drive bobbin or Irish tension lead spinning wheel: Common amongst novices because the strong pull makes it simpler to learn the "feel" for managing the amount of twist to add. They're also perfect for bulkier yarns because of the strong draw. Irish tension spinning wheels are preferred by some since they treadle the quickest. Fine yarns may necessitate more skill and practice. Incredibly sharp yarns could be tough to work with on Irish tension.

Single drive flyer or Scotch tension lead spinning wheel: These are excellent all-around performers and work very well with extremely fine yarns. The brake may be set so that the bobbin spins with the flyer even when just lightly pulled, making it excellent for ultrafine yarn. You can as well make some adjustments to the bobbin to pull stronger for thicker yarns. Scotch tension wheels are popular and versatile.

Double drive spinning wheels: It's almost as though they're on autopilot. Both the bobbin and the flyer are spun without tension. The bobbin spins quicker, allowing you to wind yarn while using the flyer to create a twist. You can alter the amount of twist added by using various "pulleys" to allow the bobbin to spin a bit or "a lot" faster (see "ratios" below). You may also utilize Scotch tension to make the bobbin "slip" and spin with the flyer to add an extra twist. It's a little tough to adjust how readily the bobbin slips, but it's simple once you get the hang of it. It's a lot of fun spinning finer and moderate yarns on double drive wheels.

Several double drive wheels can be converted to single-drive Scotch tension; thus, a double drive wheel is a smart choice if you want Scotch tension or double drive. Overall, this is a pretty versatile setup.

Drive Ratios

Consider ratios to be the gears on a bicycle. Ratios indicate the speed at which your flyer or bobbin spins in comparison to the speed at which you treadle your drive wheel. For spinning varied weight yarns, drive ratios are critical: Bulky yarns have low (slow) ratios, while finer yarns have high (quick) ratios.

A typical low ratio is 4, 4:1, or "4 to 1." This simply implies that every time the driving wheel revolves once, the bobbin or flyer rotates four times each. A high ratio could be anything from 10:1 and 30:1.

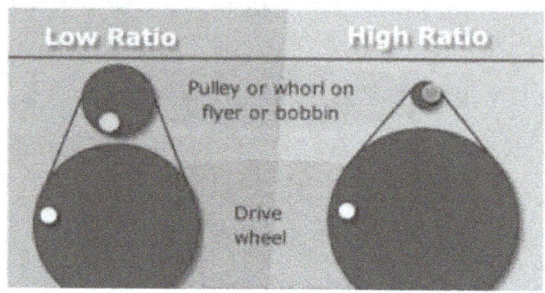

You can alter the ratios! Simply vary the size of the pulley or whorl. Slower spin is associated with a greater pulley or whorl. Low ratios are simpler to treadle on a spinning wheel, just like low gears, which can easily be peddled on a bicycle.

Drive Ratios: The Verdict

Fortunately, most wheels can handle a large variety of ratios and are suitable for regularly spun yarns. Opt for a wheel with a high ratio range if you'll be spinning fine fibers. Opt for a wheel with a low range ratio if you'll work with bulky yarns.

The Extras

It turns out that spinning is about more than just the wheel! Is there a set of spare bobbins, whorls, or flyers included with the wheel? What about a Lazy Kate (a bobbin stand that's great when you want to ply spun fibers into multi-ply yarns)? Is there a carrying case included?

New or used

Buying a Pre-used Spinning Wheel

Many people do not have sufficient capital to opt for a new wheel. In this case, one can opt for a used wheel because your first purchase might not appear as your lifetime favorite, no matter the amount of research you put into getting the wheel.

Before purchasing a used wheel, ensure the brand you select is one in which the spare parts and extra bobbins are readily available. If not, you might spend extra on purchasing handmade spare bobbins. The Ashford brand makes sure you get all the parts and bobbins required off the shelf.

Also, you should be careful when purchasing a used wheel from e-commerce sites. Using eBay, for example, you may not really tell what a wheel is like from just a photograph. You can always make a wild guess, especially with affordable prices, but this option is not the safest.

This is also applicable to second-hand and antique shop bargains. Try a wheel out before purchasing it, or get a friend with experience to inspect the wheel for you.

Below are a few places you can get good spinning wheels:

- Flea Markets

- Antique and used goods stores

- eBay

- Estate sales/auctions

Buying a Shiny New Wheel

If you have enough capital, you can purchase a brand new spinning wheel, but you should test as many wheels as possible. Visit a vendor close by and sample some wheels before making your final choice.

Three factors to consider when shopping for a new spinning wheel are:

1. Do you have any physical challenges that could need special attention? When choosing a wheel, your height should also be considered; you need to decide whether your wheel orifice/flyer should be lower or higher.

2. Do you desire a portable wheel? This question is important as you may need it to travel for workshops and shows.

3. What position do you want your flyer to be in? Do you want it on the right or left of the wheel? Or do you want an upright one?

One other thing you need to put into consideration is the orifice size. This also affects the kind of yarn you spin on the machine. Some wheels are available with additional plastic to make their feed hole smaller, more important when you're using fine yarns.

This next tip is for lovers of list. First of all, form a list outlining all the factors you like (price, double thread, modern design, bobbin brake, etc.). Then navigate to the manufacturer's page and look for the wheels that meet your needs. Include them in your list, then give points to each of them according to category (e.g., design points, price points, brake points, etc.). In conclusion, add up all the points to see the wheel that fits the factors the most.

Also, take the types of accessories available into consideration. Some spinning wheels provide more accessories than others. These accessories could consist of larger bobbins, fast-spinning whorls, attachable reels, etc.). These accessories can add much to your spinning wheel. So you can make this a factor to consider when buying your wheel.

Types of Spinning Wheels

There are many options to pick from because the market is flooded with different sorts of spinning wheels. If you're interested in knowing the various types of spinning wheels, then read along.

Charka Wheels

The infamous "Charka" was brought by Gandhi in India with plans to help the people of his country gain independence and self-sufficiency. And it was quite successful.

This machine does not need a bobbin or flyer to work. While working on this device, you have to use one hand to rotate the round disk and, with the other, draft the fiber to produce a smooth yarn.

Example

Box-style and Table-top Charkas.

Application

Basically, Chakra is used to make comfortable fabrics. It could also be used for making traditional fabrics like khaddar, angora, cashmere, cotton, silk, etc.

Electric Spinner Wheel

This type doesn't have wheels, so calling it a "Spinning Wheel" is not fair.

It does, however, have a flyer, which aids in the even winding of yarn onto the bobbins. These spinners' tiny size makes them ideal for setting up on a table and in a small space!

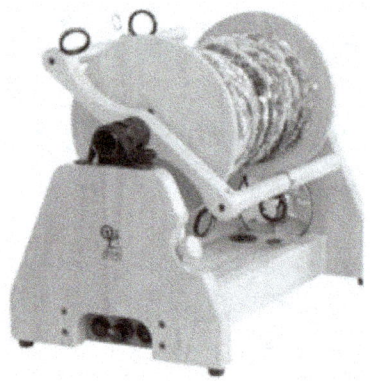

The best thing is that you get to experience all of the benefits of a regular machine without worrying about manually adjusting the speed ratio because it does it for you.

Example

Ashford Electric Spinner, Roberta, etc.

Application

This device is ideal for persons who do not want to treadle, particularly those who are unable to move much owing to physical restrictions.

Saxony Wheel

It is also known as the "Cinderella Wheel" as it is commonly found in fairytales.

The device's components are positioned horizontally, with the huge hoop on one end and the flyer on the other. It also has a slanting frame and usually three legs to keep it upright on the ground.

Example

Ashford Traditional, Elizabeth 2, Polonaise, Schacht-Reeves, etc.

Application

This machine is commonly used to make fine to moderate thread or yarns from fiber. It's also rather simple to use, making it an excellent alternative for beginners.

Norwegian Spinning Wheel

It's actually fairly similar to the machine we previously discussed. The main difference is that instead of three legs, it has four to support its bench-like frame.

The machine is supported by a table with a horizontal build-up. It's directly next to the flyer, and it's occasionally paired with a tiny upper table for your convenience.

Example

Kromski Spinning Wheel.

Application

This machine can do nearly all of the functions of the Saxony machine. In both little and large quantities, it's utilized to make linen, fine wool, and other popular fibers.

Castle Wheel

The key characteristic that sets the Castle machine apart is its vertical-shaped design. The purpose behind this cleverly-built architecture is that it takes the least floor space compared to the other devices mentioned in this article!

This machine also comes with different speed ratios for you to choose from and you can control how many twists you want to put into the yarn as per your preference.

Example

Ashford Traveller, Majacraft wheel.

Application

This is probably the only machine out there that lets you get away with almost ALL sorts of experimental materials like paper, silk or even fabric scraps and produces a great result in the end!

Modern Wheel

Everything changes over time, including these machines!

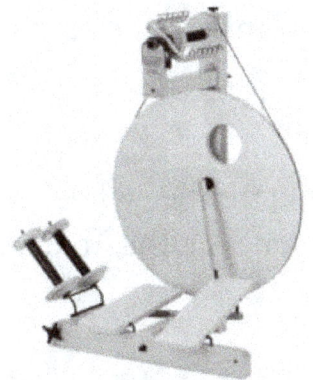

Some machines are developed using modern technology to improve their aesthetics and efficiency in order to maximize productivity and performance.

These machines are classified as a hybrid version because they blend old and modern systems in such a way that best serves the user's needs.

Example

Kromski Sonata, Ladybug, Flatiron, Ashford Joy, etc.

Application

These new spinning machines are generally more user-friendly, compact, and a few even come with portable facilities for your comfort, thanks to superior engineering systems. With the aid of this machine, you can make a variety of threads or yarns from fabric.

Great/Walking Wheel

This machine is a spindle wheel version, with the spindle serving as one of the machine's most critical components.

Walking spinners are one of the earliest creations in the world of wheels because they do not have a treadle or a flyer! So, if you enjoy antiques with historical significance, this could be the one for you.

Example

Antique Scottish Great Wheel.

Application

This machine is used to make fine threads or yarn from various fine fibers (Cotton and Silk).

To sum this section up, below are the recommended spinning wheels (brands) for beginners:

1. Ashford
2. Louet
3. Lendrum
4. Kromski

Fiber

Spinning can be done with almost anything that resembles fiber. Sheep's wool, alpaca, mohair (from angora goats), cotton, silk, and angora (from angora rabbits) are the most popular fibers used for hand spinning. Sheep's wool is, in my opinion, the easiest fiber to learn to spin, though the concepts are the same for spinning any fiber.

When choosing your first spinning fiber, there are a few factors to keep in mind.

You should first learn a little about microns. Microns are a measurement of how coarse or fine a fiber is, and they usually range from 18 to 35 microns. The number indicates how much "grip" the fiber has, and the lesser the value, the finer and more "loose" the fiber is. A fiber with a low micron count is understandably difficult for a beginner spinner to control. A micron count in the mid-20s to low-30s will provide enough grip to prevent the fiber from falling off your hands while still allowing you to draft the fiber to spin it.

Next, you will need to consider the staple length. Individual fiber length or an average length in a mix of fibers is referred to as staple length. The lengths can range from less than one inch to more than seven inches. It's crucial to understand since, in general, the shorter the staple length, the more challenging it is to spin. This is due to the fact that short fibers require more twists for the yarn to take, which can be tough for inexperienced spinners to achieve consistently. A fiber with a staple length of 3 – 5″ is recommended for beginners. To put it another way, start with fiber that isn't fresh from the animal. You'll have lots of time to practice how to process your own raw fiber as your spinning passion progresses.

Sheep come in a variety of breeds, each of which produces distinct types of wool. It's critical to grasp the qualities and objectives of the various varieties so that you can predict the types of yarn they'll make. Part of becoming a skilled hand spinner is being able to choose the proper fiber for a certain goal and achieving that goal successfully.

Wool comes in a wide range of colors, lengths, curls, and textures. Fine wools, medium / crossbred wools, and long wools are the three main varieties of wool.

Fine Wools

This wool type has the softest fiber diameter of the other wool varieties, ranging from 50 to 90 microns. Fine wools spin into fine yarns that are perfect for knitting and crocheting crafts. They're great for making clothing that can be worn against the skin, particularly infant wearables. Fine wools combine beautifully with other exotic fibers like alpaca, mohair, camel, silk, angora and so on, adding elasticity and loft.

Merino

- Is the softest and finest of all the wool types.
- It has a fine crimp and a bright white natural color.
- It has a staple length of 2 1/2 to 4 inches and has a high grease content.
- Good felting wool
- Works best when spun fine
- Challenging for beginners to spin due to how soft and short the fibers are

Rambouillet

- 2–4 inch staple length
- Challenging for beginners to spin due to how soft and short the fibers are
- More flexibility
- Most loft

- Works best when spun fine
- Spins woolen or worsted yarns

Medium / Crossbred Wools

These wools are best-suited for hand spinners who are just starting out. They are versatile wool that spins into a medium-thick yarn suitable for crocheted, knitted, and woven garments and materials.

Coopworth, Corriedale, Jacob, Romney, Blue Faced Leicester, Border Leicester

- Merino wool crossbred
- Mildly soft
- 3–5 inch staple length
- Easy to spin for beginners
- Great for felting
- Spins medium-thick yarn
- Spins woolen or worsted yarn

Long Wools

These wools are used to make worsted yarns for woven and knitted outerwear that are robust and glossy.

Because the long-staple of fiber can tangle while spinning, spinning from the fold is the perfect option.

Lincoln Longwool, Wensleydale, and the Cotswolds

- Moderate to coarse texture
- Very robust, durable
- Wavy crimp
- Lustrous to semi-lustrous
- 5 – 8 1/2 inch staple length
- Easy to spin for inexperienced hand spinners
- Resembles mohair
- Not well suitable for felting
- Wear resistant
- Spin medium-thick yarn
- Combines well with other long-staple fibers, such as mohair
- Excellent for worsted and semi-worsted yarn

Down Wools

Because these wools have a short-staple, they are not suitable for beginning hand spinners. Down wools come in several diameters, from soft to medium. Soft fleeces are utilized in clothing such as socks and fine textiles. Knitted and woven clothing, long-wearing clothing, and blankets can all benefit from the medium-range fleeces.

Dorset, Suffolk, Cheviot, Shetland

- Fine to medium texture
- Spiral crimp
- Lofty, spongy, crisp
- 2–3 1/2 inch staple length
- Very durable
- Tough to spin for inexperienced hand spinners
- Lacks luster, chalky
- Excellent shape retention
- Not well suitable for felting
- Wear resistant
- Spin medium-thick yarn
- To increase resilience, pair with long wool fiber.

Types of Processed and Unprocessed Fibers

1. Top

Top is fiber that has been combed through a wool comb, which resembles a huge hair comb. True top is hand-processed, with all the fibers moving in the same orientation (direction) and little air between them. Worsted yarns (not worsted weight, but worsted style) are spun by traditional spinners using top.

2. Commercial Top

This is top but, in this case, machine-made. But, just in case you needed any more proof that humans are superior to machines (at least for the time being), this processed version isn't quite as good as the handcrafted one. In commercial tops, nearly all fibers run in the same direction (notice that we mentioned nearly), and much of the air between the fibers have been removed.

3. Roving

Wool that has been run via a mill on a carding machine is known as roving. A carding machine has teeth that brush the fiber (much like a huge hairbrush) so that it mostly goes in the same orientation. However, the texture will be fuzzier than the top because roving fibers do not all go in the same orientation.

Woolen style yarn, or simply "woolen," is what you get when you spin roving into yarn, even if it isn't comprised of wool. (Yes, it's perplexing!) Because of the air between the fibers, it produces a light, fluffy yarn.

Because the fibers aren't completely aligned, they can easily cling onto each other during the felting process. Roving is also a fantastic fiber for needle felting.

4. Rolags

Fiber that has been processed with hand cards or a blending board is called rolag.

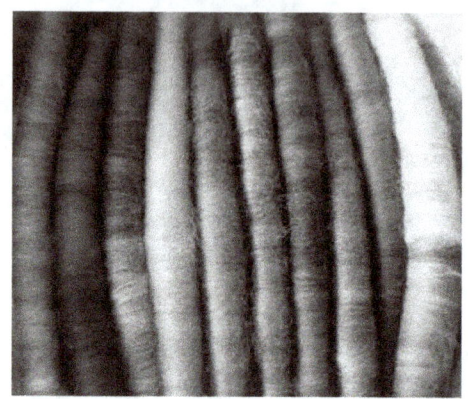

The fibers are either combed through on the cards or dragged across the board, then wrapped by hand into long rolls. Rolags are similar to slimmer, lengthier versions of art batts (see below), and they're great for spinning moderate, textured yarns — thick or thin.

5. Batts

Fibers that have been processed on a drum carder, which looks like a huge round hairbrush with a handle, are called batts. Fibers are inserted into the handle and brushed and mixed.

Many fiber artists enjoy creating art batts with lots of texture, color, and sparkle. The fibers are enjoyable to spin, producing substantial thick and thin yarns with lots of beautiful diversity and random-looking pieces.

6. Wool Locks

These are washed and occasionally dyed fibers that may be isolated into separate locks from the sheep. You may either spin straight from the wool locks or use a drum carder to generate an art batt for extra texture.

You can also use hand combs to transform them into true tops. Wool locks are an unprocessed kind of fiber that can be transformed into any of the above-mentioned forms already discussed.

7. Raw Wool

This fiber type is shorn from sheep but hasn't been processed in any way. Some spinners prefer to spin "in the grease," straight from the raw fleece. To spin in the grease, you will need a very clean, heavily skirted fleece. Alternatively, you can wash the fleece and use it to make any of the forms listed above.

By the way, the terms "combed" and "carded" are occasionally used interchangeably. These terms simply refer to fiber that has been combed or carded with wool combs or carders. Wool combs are like combs, while carders are like hairbrushes.

You will want to use roving, which is sheep's wool that has been cleaned to remove excess lanolin (grease) and combed or carded to align each fiber in the same direction. Roving is available at your local yarn store or from a number of online retailers such as etsy.com and woolery.com. Try to stay away from "top" for the time being, which is wool that has been combed to remove all but the longest strands, making things more complicated for the beginner, though it is fun to spin once you've gained a little experience via constant practice!

Note for Beginners

I strongly advise beginners to start with a purchase of 100 percent wool roving if they have never spun before. However, there is a particular type of roving called pencil roving, which is roving that has been pre-drafted for you. What exactly does this imply? Pulling the fibers away in creating a thin, even yarn is called drafting.

Most fiber preparations require drafting while you spin. Pencil roving, on the other hand, eliminates this step, allowing you to become accustomed to simply feeling the fiber spin between your fingertips — and allowing the spun yarn to wrap over your drop spindle or bobbin.

Once you've mastered pencil roving, you may move on to drafting different fiber preparations and spinning them into yarns; however, you can determine how much of this process you want to do yourself if you have your own fiber animals. Everything can be done yourself. Visit a local fiber farm or business and have a conversation with the owners. They will surely be delighted to assist you in finding something ideal for a beginner spinner. Some people pay to have their fiber shorn and then taken to a fiber mill to be washed, carded, and colored. Sending a smelly, greasy wool fleece away and receiving a box of clean, fluffy ready-to-spin wool back sounds almost magical; It's just as magical, if not more so, to experience and comprehend each phase of the process as it happens. The choice is yours; however, this book focuses on wool roving that has been processed.

Additional Tools (Optional)

Distaff

A distaff is a hand spinning tool. It's built to hold unspun fibers and to keep them untangled, thus making spinning easier. A piece of ribbon or string is used to wrap the fiber around the distaff and secure it in place.

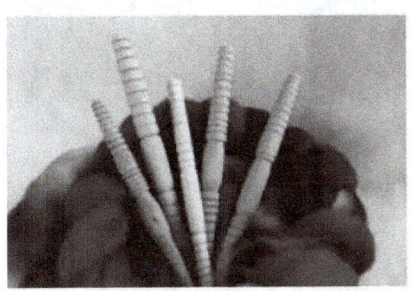

Depending on the spinning procedure, there were two popular types of distaffs. The traditional form is where a staff is held underneath the arm while the spindle is used. It's around 3 feet (0.9 m) long and is held underneath the left arm with the left hand pulling the fibers out. This is the earliest of the two forms of distaff since spinning on a spindle originated before spinning on a whee.

You can also use a distaff as a spinning wheel accessory. It's beside the bobbin on a wheel so that the spinner can get to it conveniently. The spindle version is longer than this one; however, they are identical.

Niddy Noddy

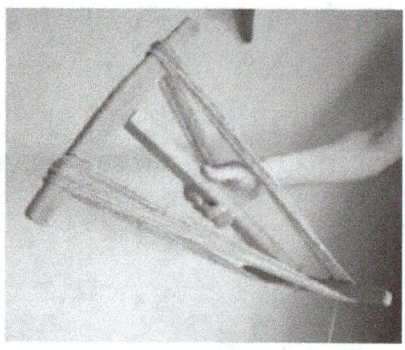

A niddy-noddy is used for making yarn skeins. It is made up of a center bar with crossbars at every end, 90 degrees apart. To make it simpler to hold, the center bar is usually carved. One of the crossbars will either be totally removed or have an edge that's flat for the skein to slip off. Niddy-noddies are made from a variety of materials, including metal, wood, and plastic. Wood is a traditional material, and most high-quality niddy-noddies are still constructed of it. Conservative spinners sometimes employ PVC pipe niddy-noddies.

Nostepinne

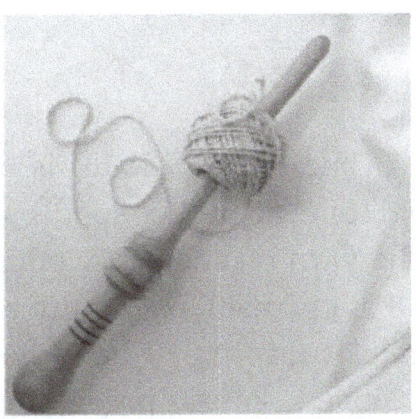

Also called a nostepinde, is a fiber arts tool that is used to wind yarn; usually, hand spun yarn into a ball for crocheting, knitting, or weaving. The most common material is wood, which can be twisted around with yarn. Nostepinnes with decorative and intricate carvings are widespread. The top of the nostepinne has a notch that allows one of the yarn's ends to be held tight, whereas the others are twisted into a ball. A nostepinne makes a "center pull" ball that allows the working yarn to be taken by a knitter from the ball's center instead of outside. This increases knitting stability and ensures the working yarn does not roll about on the surface it is sitting on. Due to their cylindrical, short shape, these center-pull balls are referred to as "cakes."

Lazy Kate

A lazy kate (also known as a kate) is a tool used in spinning to hold one or more spools or bobbins in position while the yarn on them is wound off from the bobbin's side. A kate is made up of numerous rods that allow the bobbins to spin. A band loops over the bobbins on tensioned kates, preventing them from spinning freely. Built-in kates are available on some spinning wheels, but they are more difficult to use than free-standing kates.

Kates are often used to ply yarn, but they can also be used for any task that requires winding yarn off a bobbin.

While a wooden kate like the one shown above is far more durable, a similar effect may be produced using cardboard boxes and dowels.

Pre-Drafting Fiber

Pre-drafting may be necessary, depending on how your fiber arrives—thinning out your fiber before drafting is called pre-drafting. Previously, I mentioned that with pencil roving, you wouldn't need to pre-draft the fiber because it has already been pre-drafted; however, in this section, I will discuss how to pre-draft fiber just in case you couldn't lay your hands on pencil roving.

Many fibers are packed too heavily to allow for easy and even pulling of the fibers to spin. So you've to pre-draft. This could be done by breaking a wool braid into lengths first. Then you'll need to pull those lengths into thinner pieces. To make the wool fibers even thinner, you can go through these strips and gently tug them in portions. Pulling fiber via a tool with a small hole to thin it out is another pre-drafting procedure. This is normally done when you have a ball of fiber or if you have leftover or unprepared fibers that you want to straighten out. It is entirely dependent on how you obtain your fiber.

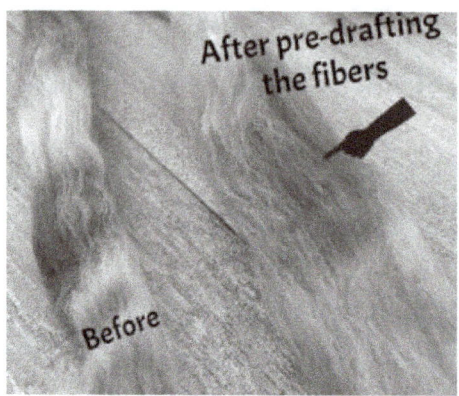

There will be some fibers that are longer than others. The longer they are, the better and the easier it will be to pre-draft them because there will be more connections to make. When I deal with shorter lengths, I found that pre-drafting makes it much easier for me to break the length when thinning out the material. It happens all the time. It's quite simple to fix. I prefer to break the fibers on each broken end and feed them together, then swiftly spin them before they separate. Some felt it a little to keep it together, while others simply laid the ends together before spinning, knowing that they would mend during the remainder of the yarn's processing.

Drafting Fibre For Consistent Yarn

I'm fairly convinced that if you're learning to spin your own yarn, you've struggled to get a constant thickness. When it comes to producing a consistent handspun yarn, there are several aspects to consider, which we shall explore in a bit.

Drafting is dependent on how you obtain your fiber. A rolag, for example, is a sheet of carded fiber that has been rolled after being removed from the carding machine. It isn't always necessary to pre-draft and can be taken straight off the roll as you spin. Drafting is the process of drawing fibers apart so that air and twist can be added and the fiber may be turned into yarn as you feed your fiber to your drop spindle or spinning wheel. Some people prefer to hold their prepared materials using a distaff. As you spin, you can gently pull off the fiber. As you draft, it seems almost cloud-like, and the fibers look like spiderwebs. Thinning out pre-drafted materials with your fingertips while you work is another drafting approach.

The guidelines for consistent drafting will undoubtedly be beneficial to you, so let's jump right into it.

1. All Thumbs

Thumbs are far more crucial than one may imagine in maintaining consistent spinning. Stopping the twist from going past your thumb and into the source of fiber is critical. If this happens, you'll end up with a large, tangled mess that you'll have to untangle. If this happens, use your fingers to untwist the fiber and pinch it again. It's worth noting that a death hold isn't required; just enough to prevent the twist from passing through.

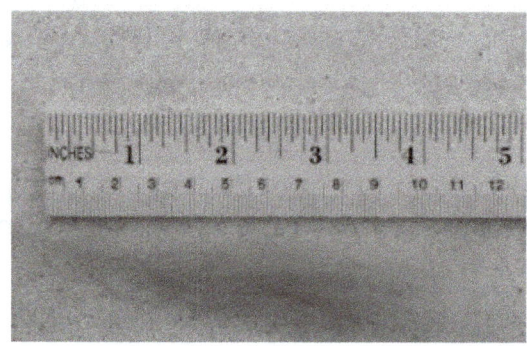

2. Staple Length

To begin, determine the length of your fiber's staples and divide that number by two. You might wonder why. Because I know my staple length here is around 4 and 5", and that if half that length is drafted, I should never get just one end of the fibers (causing a thin spot) or a huge clump in the middle (causing a thick spot known as a slub, see below), which means I should always maintain a consistent thickness of fibers in my drafting zone.

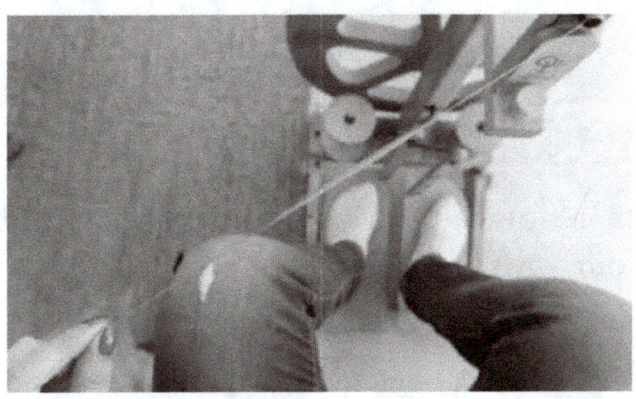

3. Know Your Drafting Triangle

The actual shape at the end of the fiber when you draft from it is referred to as the drafting triangle. As the fibers are slowly pulled apart, they will form a triangle. To help with consistency, always grab the fiber from the drafting triangle in the same location (indicating how far down the triangle you begin to pull).

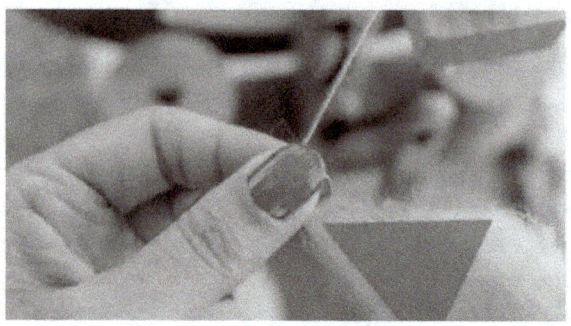

The further down the triangle you grip the fiber, the denser your yarn will be.

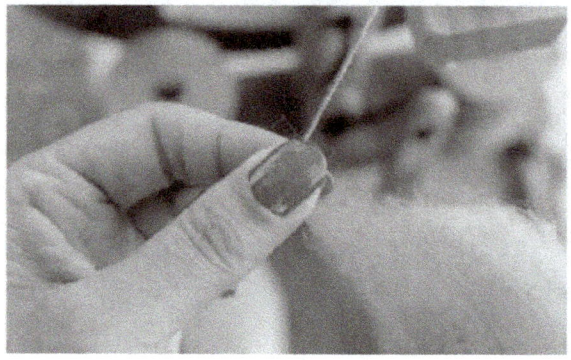

This requires no more than practice and ensures that you always begin drafting that section with the same amount of fiber.

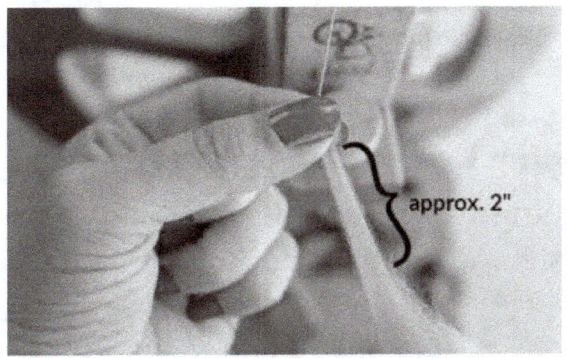

approx. 2"

Recall the staple length tip earlier discussed?

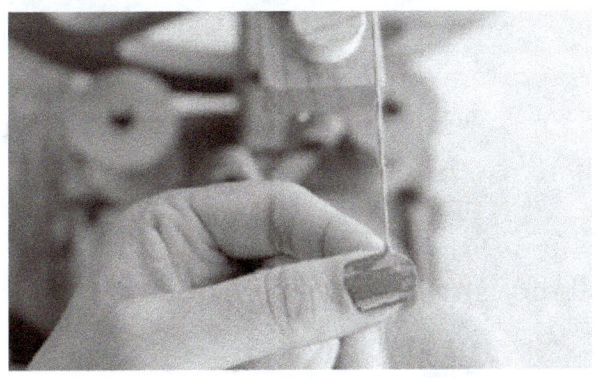

I've slid my thumb down the fiber that has been drafted, enabling the built-up twist to go down the fiber that is drafted. Now I'm ready to re-grasp the fiber, this time from the same location on the drafting triangle and pull about 2".

It's also worth noting that the twist will always tend to the fiber's thinnest point. If the yarn grows too thin or has far too much twist, it may snap. If you notice a thin place, add more fiber to that area and continue spinning as usual.

Yarn Spinning Using A Drop Spindle

Drop spinning has a number of benefits over spinning on a full-size spinning wheel. It provides you more control over the process as a beginner, allowing you to spin as slowly as you need to understand the nuances of drafting fiber, developing twist (energy), and eventually spinning a beautiful, balanced yarn. Even if you're an experienced spinner, you might choose a drop spindle for a variety of purposes, including flexibility and simplicity of usage.

I'm utilizing Romney fiber and a spindle with a top whorl to demonstrate.

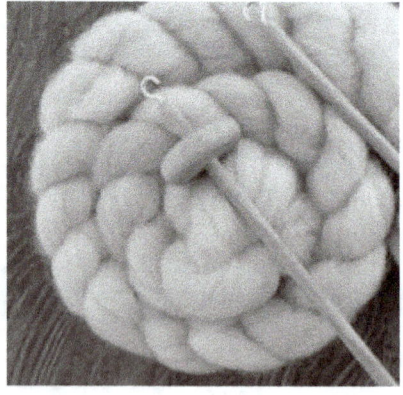

Benefits Of Using A Drop Spindle

1. You can exercise greater influence in the drafting process.

2. Capable of spinning less faster than a wheel.

3. Excellent for beginners to learn the process.

Considerations On a Drop Spindle

1. Leader or no leader?

You must first decide if you want to use a leader or not. A leader is a lengthy piece of yarn, string, or other material that is attached to the spindle's shaft, allowing you to start all over. It's also fine if you don't want a leader to start with. In the demonstration below, I'm using a piece of roving to start with, one that has been twisted to prevent it from breaking. Here's how it works:

Draft a little fiber from the roving carefully.

Continue twisting till you notice the yarn has started forming.

The yarn you just made should be hooked and start to spin it backward (on itself). Spin the spindle facing you; it should be rotating clockwise if you look at it downward.

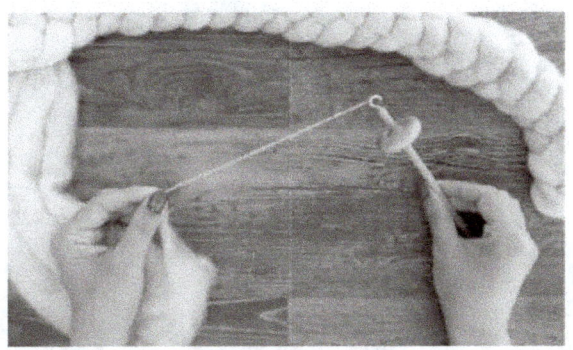

You will notice that it's a strand of yarn, doubled back upon itself and twisted a little more.

You are set to begin spinning, given that you now have some leader fiber!

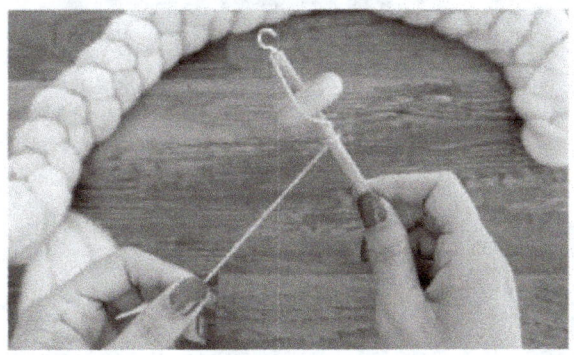

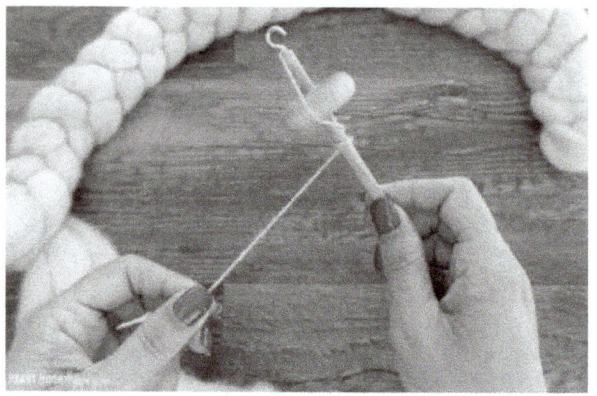

A little more of the fiber should be twisted around the shaft, just beneath the whorl.

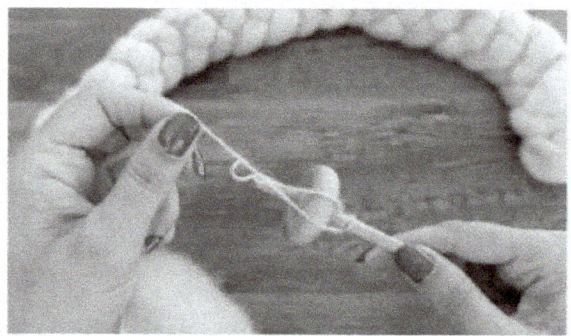

Bring back up the yarn over the whorl, and wound it twice across the hook. This ensures it does not slip off while spinning.

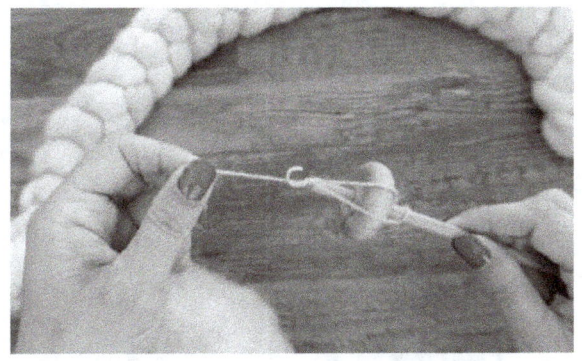

Now, you are prepared to commence the spinning process.

Tip: I noticed that leaving a good 4 – 5" of yarn over the hook after wounding helps with consistency, so don't wrap everything you have around the shaft.

2. Park and draft or suspended spinning?

A drop spindle can be used in two ways: park and draft or suspended spinning.

Beginners prefer the park and draft technique, which involves having to spin the spindle (clockwise if you look at it downward) till a sufficient twist has formed in the yarn that's already spun between your thumb and the hook. When you have many twists, "park" the spindle somewhere - beneath your thigh, beneath your arm, between your feet, etc. – and draft the fibers slowly.

An example of parking the spindle between your feet

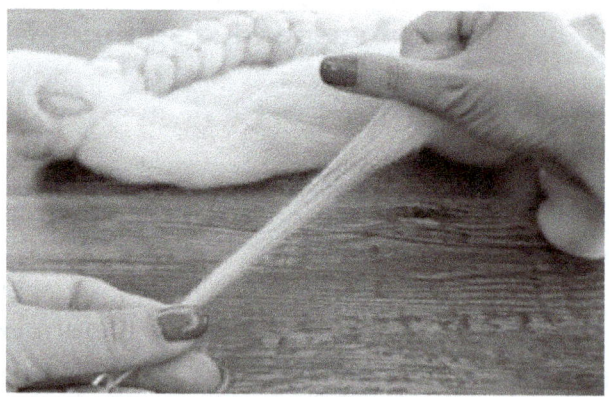

An example of drafting out fibers after parking the spindle

You'll can now proceed to suspended spinning as your spinning and drafting skills improve. This implies that as you draft the fibers, the spindle will spin along with them. It's similar to caressing your stomach and stroking your head simultaneously, so it'll take some practice. As a result, beginners prefer the park and draft approach!

Here's how:

As you can see, I've built up several additional twists in the photo below. The spindle was spun until my yarn had an extra twist. (Here, your thumb's responsibility is to keep the twist from entering the fiber.) Now I'll delicately use my roving to draft fiber and allow the twist (energy) to move up.

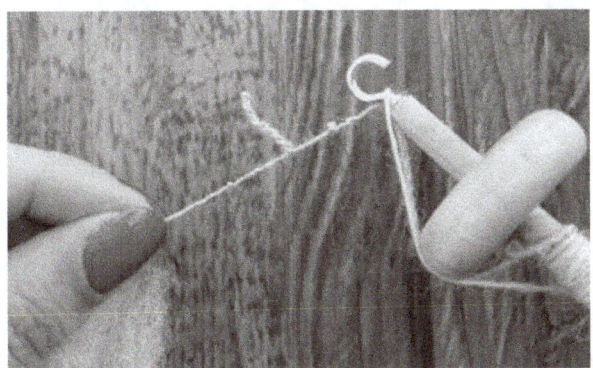

My left thumb is being positioned in a way that it prevents the twist from passing through it. Observe how releasing my right thumb enables the surplus twist to move up the fibers already drafted, releasing energy and converting it to yarn.

Folding your yarn back on itself and letting it hang is a good way to evaluate if it has enough twists. This is referred to as a ply back test, used to determine how underspun or kinky your single is. Since your single will loosen a little in the process of plying, you'd want it to be a ittle kinky. It's preferable for it to be too kinky (even if it's a little) than not being kinky enough.

I'm set to start spinning the spindle once more in building up an additional twist for the subsequent stretch of fiber once there's no more built-up twist. If the yarn between your thumb and the hook is long enough (approaching your arm's span), detach the hook from the spindle, twist it over the shaft, and take it back up, hook it over the hook two times to stop it from moving around while you spin.

You'll keep repeating this procedure till you've exhausted the source of your fiber. If you want to take a break, just wound the fiber/ yarn over the shaft/ hook a couple of times extra until you are set to pick it up again.

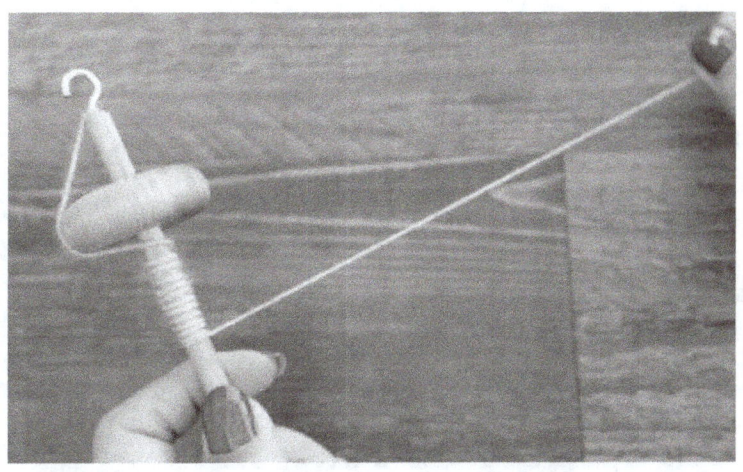

To make the spindle spin faster, I begin at my right knee and have the shaft rolled up to my thigh, allowing it to spin freely till it feels kinky before parking it.

Use your thumb in drafting the fibers as a gateway, allowing the twist to move up them. Remember that consistency is key, and using a drop spindle to make your yarn is a pleasant and affordable means to get started. It's worth noting that your yarn needs to be plied before using it. This will reinforce the yarn and prevent it from unraveling.

Yarn Spinning Using A Wheel

Assemble Your Wheel and Get It Ready to Spin

To begin, make sure your wheel is fully assembled, along with all of the necessary nuts and bobs, as well as the drive band. It makes no difference what kind of wheel you have. These instructions apply to any treadle wheel with a flyer, whether it's a double drive, single drive, double treadle, or single treadle. The fundamentals of spinning remain the same.

Treadling

Next is to treadle air, which may seem counterintuitive. That's correct, I want you to sit down, remove your shoes, and treadle without spinning a single fiber. Then I'd like you to treadle a little more. Treadle until you're confident enough in your wheel that you can stop it without using your hands, and that you can also start it in either direction without using your hands. It will take some time to get the hang of it, but your future spinning self will appreciate you for it.

Tips For Treadling

Keep your toes as flat as possible. You will have more control over the wheel if you flex your ankle rather than your toe.

When treadling, it's critical to maintain a steady action. You want your wheel to continue moving forward rather than moving backward.

Looking at your footman (the rod/stick attached to the hub of the wheel) will tell you the direction the wheel will turn. You'll be spinning the wheel to the right (clockwise), or a Z twist if the footman is to the right of center. If the footman is to the left of the center, you'll be spinning the wheel in the opposite direction (counterclockwise), or an S twist.

N.B: Discussions on Z and S twist are covered in subsequent sections of this chapter

Getting The Wheel Set For Spinning

You'll need a new bobbin and a lengthy piece of yarn to begin. (Really, any yarn will do; we're just using it as a "leader" to get the bobbin going.)

The yarn should be folded in half and fastened around the bobbin. Make certain it's secure.

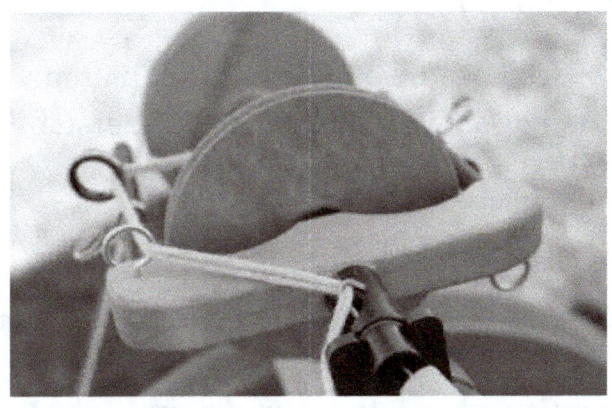

Thread the leader yarn through the hook's top (or across the yarn guide, as I did) on one of the flyer's arms. Pull it via the orifice (if one exists) using your threading hook.

Adjusting Tension

Right now, we'll go through the fundamentals of wheel tension. To begin, you must first understand how to tighten and relax the tension on your wheel.

Double Drive

For a double drive wheel, the tension control is typically a knob that you crank to move the flyer assembly farther from or closer to your driving wheel. Moving away increases your double drive band tension, causing your yarn to pull harder. As you get nearer to the drive wheel, your double drive band's tension and the pull on your yarn will altogether reduce.

Single Drive

A single drive system may feature a knob, screw, or another type of lever for adjustments. Increase or decrease a break band or strap situated over your bobbin (bobbin lead or Scotch tension) or situated over your flyer (flyer led or Irish tension) to facilitate the adjustment of the single drive system's tension. When tension is increased on a single drive system, the tension band is tightened, generating additional resistance across the bobbin or flyer. When you decrease the tension, you are simply lowering your bobbin or flyer's tension.

Test The Tension

Place the bobbin break on the bobbin and check to ensure the tension is appropriate. To accomplish this, begin treadling while increasing the leader yarn's twist. The following are signs of good tension:

1. The leader should be picked up by the bobbin with some considerable force, but not with an excessive force that it pulls it apart from your hand.

2. It would be possible for the leader to be pulled back out with little effort and the bobbin being able to resume picking up the leader as soon as pulling is stopped (by you).

You may have a tension that's too tight if you can't take the leader away from the bobbin as you keep a slow spin. Additionally, if you can pick up some noise, this could be an indication of excessive tension. Try again after the break on the bobbin is loosened a little.

The leader will not be taken up by the bobbin if there isn't enough tension. Instead, you'll observe that the yarn/ leader will merely spin and kink while remaining stationary. In this case, the tension on your bobbin should be tightened and double-checked to ensure that the yarn/ leader hasn't gotten trapped on a hook or is otherwise obstructed.

Getting Started

You're set to start using your fiber for spinning once you've discovered the tension balance that's suitable for your wheel.

Choose the hand you'll use to manage the twist (forward hand) and the hand to manipulate the fiber before you start spinning (back hand).

I recommend a clean, well-prepared fiber to begin with such as roving, which is the best way to learn (we have covered different types of wool in the previous section, so kindly revisit them). For the time being, stay away from raw fleece and locks. Although, if you are an experienced spinner, you can also use well-blend batts or top, but for a beginner spinner, roving would do just fine. Rolags could also be used, but I prefer to use them for spinning with a long draw technique (woolen style), which I see as a little more sophisticated to kick off with, except you are an experienced spinner.

The drafting technique used below is the short draw technique which turns roving into worsted yarn. The term "short draw" alludes to the fact that you feed the fiber into the wheel with your hands close together. The twist is added by the hand nearest to the wheel.

Start spinning the wheel clockwise because the Z twist is used to spin most singles, whereas the S twist is used to ply them.

The leader should be attached to the source of your fiber by introducing the small flyaway fibers perpendicularly into the twist on the leader and allowing some build-up twist to occur. Use your front hand to pull the source of your fiber forward, but not too much for it to break. This is only a matter of practice, so go slowly at first. Proceed at a rate you're comfortable with. If you follow the above recommendations, the freshly twisted yarn will softly pull away from your hand. The wheel should be allowed to do the heavy lifting.

Ensure your hand is not sliding or rubbing down the length of the fibers. Instead, pinch, draft a little fiber from its source, then let go, pinch, draft a little fiber, then let go, allowing the yarn that has been spun to feed onto the bobbin. The pinch, draft, and let go process should be repeated until you have a full bobbin or have exhausted your spinning fiber.

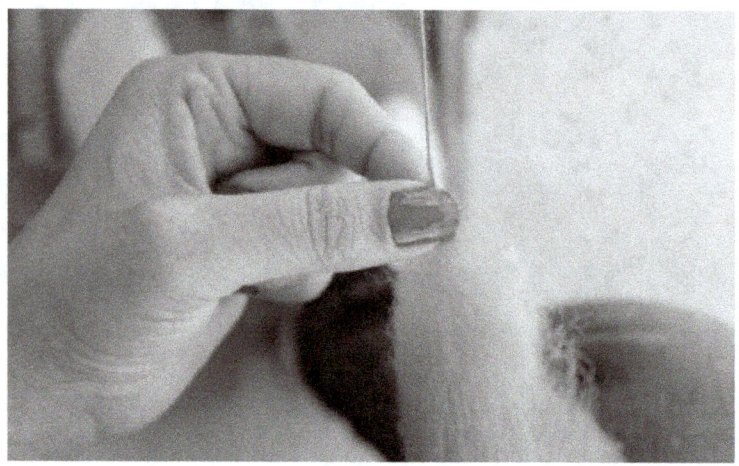

Things To Remember

Keep your hands active at all times. You risk generating so many twists that it eats into the source of your fiber if your hands stop working without halting the wheel.

The rear hand is in charge of the fiber, and you should aim at drawing and twisting from the triangle at the end of it. More information on how to obtain constant spinning has been discussed previously under "Drafting Fiber for Consistent Spinning."

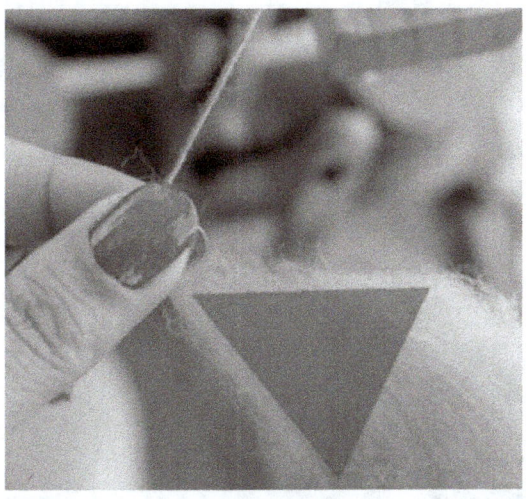

Twist will pass over the thick areas and accumulate in the thin areas. It will be easier to avoid this if you practice consistent drafting.

The thickness of the yarn is directly proportional to the amount of fiber in the drafting zone. Remember that your completed yarn, after plying, should be at least twice as thick as the single.

It's preferable to have a little more twists than when you don't have sufficient twists. A section of the twists will be gone after plying.

If the wheel spins faster than your hands, it will take up lots of twists, leaving you with an overspun yarn (as shown below) or being unable to manage the transfer of the twist to the source of your fiber, leading to a thick mess. Ensure you go slowly. (I know I've said it before, but it's important!) The worst-case scenario is that the wheel will not spin fast enough, forcing you to exercise patience for the proper quantity of twist to develop before you feed it onto the bobbin.

Inspecting Your Twist

When hung loose, the yarn that you've freshly spun should be smooth and bouncy, not excessively kinky. A ply back test can be used to determine the number of twists in your handspun. Take out a tiny amount of freshly spun yarn (20" or so) back via the orifice, double it, and hang it. You've probably spun a good single if it doesn't hang straight and flat without lots of kinks.

Yarn Plying

Yarn ply is one of knitting's best-kept secrets. Most people aren't familiar with ply (unless they're also spinners). Twisting two or more single threads in the reverse direction from which they were spun is known as plying. The singles can be kept as a single ply yarn or from a lazy kate, you can have them plied together. Weaving and crochet projects frequently use singles. Two-plied yarns are great for knitting projects.

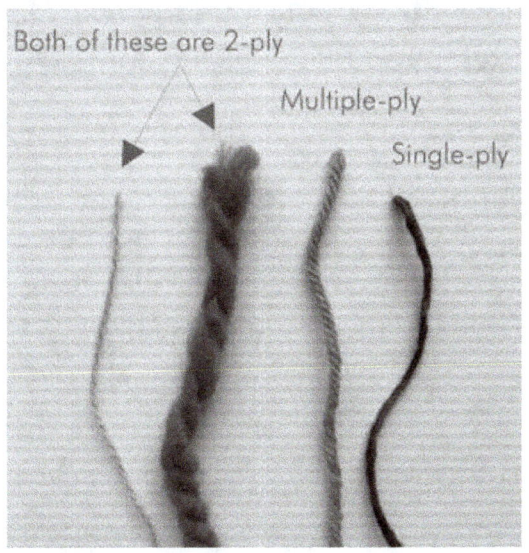

Before we begin, it's important to understand that the term "yarn plies" can refer to two different things.

What Does Ply Really Mean?

Yarn ply is a term used in the United States in describing the quantity of yarn strands that make up the final yarn.

It doesn't refer to the quantity of strands in certain other countries. It's actually describing the weight of the yarn. For instance, you would hear a yarn termed as "4 ply." This could be another way of describing a fingering weight yarn, and it has no relationship with the quantity of strands.

This is not how I use the term. However, knowing that it exists will keep you from getting confused.

Ply – If It's Not Really Twisted?

What Do I Call It?

It's called a "single" or "single ply" if the yarn isn't twisted and doesn't resemble rope.

Ply – Does It Look Like Rope?

What Should I Describe It As?

If the yarn is made up of numerous strands, it might be classified as one of several plies. Here are a few options:

- Chained ply or Navajo ply: Chain or Navajo is a plying technique for handspun yarns that works well with both dyed and undyed fibers because it doesn't interfere with colorwork. As if crocheting, the makers will produce a 200mm or 8" loop through the leader end's loop. The strands will then be twisted together in the other direction. If you do it in the reverse direction, the strands will not tangle or release rapidly. When there's just around 76mm (2 to 3 inches) of strand left in the loop, the spinner draws a new 180mm (7-inch) yarn loop through it and begins spinning. They'll repeat the process until all of the yarn has been plied.

  The fundamental benefit of this yarn plying technique is that spinners may match thin and thin spots, resulting in a smooth yarn.

- Special Yarn Ply: This plying technique produces "special effects" yarns or yarn plies, sometimes known as novelty yarns. The strands can have a variety of strand tensions, sizes, and other characteristics. Twisting a delicate, dense fiber or strand against a twisted, thin fiber or strand is a great illustration.

The core or base, effect, and binder are usually the three strands involved in the process. The base is responsible for the yarn's strength and structure, while the effect strand is responsible for the decorative detail. The effect can be anything from a loop to a knot. Finally, as the name implies, the binder will connect the base and effect strands.

Why Should I Be Concerned About Multiple Strands?

In general, the number of strands in a yarn can have an impact on multiple aspects.

Don't try to stop your yarn from doing what it's supposed to do. Even if you "get it" to perform what you want, it will almost certainly revert to its original state.

The following are some of the characteristics that ply can impact:

1. Strength

   - The strength of the plies increases as the number of plies increases. A single yarn, regardless of its weight, will not be as strong as a 3-ply yarn. You can frequently tear a single by pulling on it.

   - Singles aren't the best choice for hard-wearing items like socks or mittens, but they look great in a scarf or shawl.

2. Stitch Definition

   - A multitude of plies will usually give you a better stitch definition.

3. Roundness

   - The more the yarn is round, the more plies there are.

   - A 2-ply yarn, when used in conjunction with ribbing or cables, will commonly flatten out. It may have extra texture in stockinette than other plies.

Application of Certain Plies

Single Ply: Best for knitting that isn't put to a lot of wear and tear.

Two Ply: Mostly used in lace

Plies of three or more: Great for cables, socks, and other areas that call for the definition of stitch and strength.

Z Twist Vs S Twist

There are two types of yarn ply twists and they are Z twist and S twist.

The orientation in which your wheel or spindle spins while spinning your fiber into yarn is referred to as Z twist or S twist. A Z twist is when the wheel spins to the right (clockwise) when you gaze at it, and an S twist is when the wheel spins to the left (counter-clockwise). (If you're using a drop spindle, it's the spindle's direction as you gaze down at it.)

You might wonder what the difference is. The answer is how you ply!

Always spin in one direction and then ply the yarn in the opposing direction while spinning yarn. This helps to even out the yarn, make it stronger, and remove any additional twist from the singles. When spinning a single yarn (one bobbin), the Z twist is traditionally used. Then you'll use an S twist to ply that bobbin (either by plying more singles or a Navajo (aka Chain) ply).

Technically, however, it doesn't matter which direction you start with as long as you ply in the opposite direction from whence you spun your singles.

If you're a crocheter, for example, you might find that the opposite makes a superior working yarn. (To spin, twist S, and to ply, twist Z.) This is due to the way the yarn is wrapped around the hook as you crochet with it. This is important to me as a crocheter.

The yarn will ideally be enough for all kinds of uses if you start one way and finish the other.

How to tell which twist is which

Look at a yarn vertically to see if it was spun with an S or Z twist.

In an S twist, the fibers would either run top left to bottom right just like the one below:

From top right to bottom left like the one below is a Z twist:

You can see why the first is called an S twist and the second a Z twist if you consider the middle part of the letters S and Z. Isn't it cool?

If you look at a yarn that has already been plied and the fibers go from top left to bottom right, it was plied using the S twist and, if done correctly, was originally spun with a Z twist.

Plying With a Spinning Wheel

So you've got some newly spun yarn that needs to be plied. The good news is that you are halfway to a completed yarn, and this section will show you how to ply two (or three) single bobbins into a lovely, well-balanced yarn.

How To Ply Yarn

The Navajo (Chain) ply and the 2-ply, which we shall examine soon, are two of the most prevalent techniques to ply yarn.

Begin with evenly spun singles if you want a properly plied finished result. This means they're as near to the same thickness and twist as they possibly can be. Even for skilled spinners, this would be a miracle, so don't be too hard on yourself if they aren't. After all, we are all learning! The most effective approach to learning is to simply do it.

Some spinners prefer to let singles rest for a while before plying them. If one yarn is hyper-energetic (meaning it is "fresh" and wants to untwist) and the other is stale (meaning it has been sitting there for a long time), the yarn will be unbalanced. Some argue that there is no difference, but I believe it is worth highlighting.

Before Starting

Fill your lazy kate with the singles you want to ply first, i.e, either 2 or 3 singles.

Ensure the tails of both (or all) bobbins are faced in the same way. You don't want one bobbin spinning in one direction and the other in another direction.

Both singles (or all three) should be attached to the leader with a new bobbin. I just make a knot for simplicity.

Keep in mind that we'll ply in the other direction as the singles are spun. The singles are usually spun using a Z twist (clockwise) and plied using an S twist (counter-clockwise).

Keep your front hand near the orifice so that the twist can be directed into the yarn without over twisting it. Letting the plied yarn hang suspended for a little time to test if it will hang there neatly or curl up on itself is a good way to examine the degree of twist. (It shouldn't kink at all.)

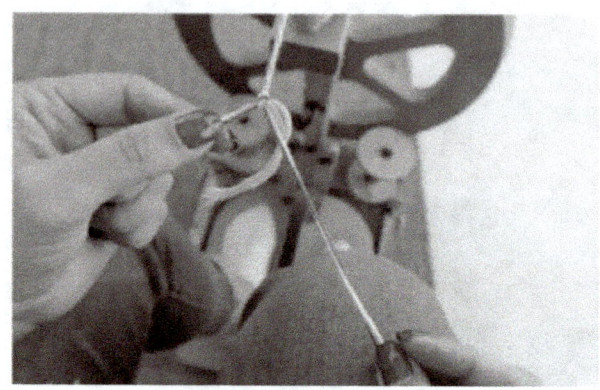

With your rear hand, ensure the two yarns are kept apart. Avoid putting your finger between the strands. Even the tiniest amount of pull on a single might cause the yarn (half of it) to be firmer when compared to the other, leading to an unstable yarn.

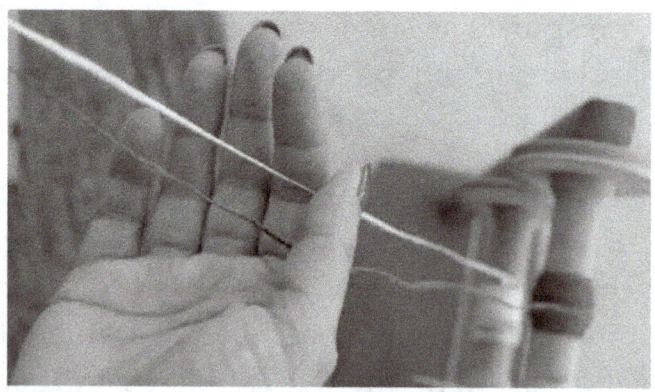

Now you will ply both singles onto a bobbin by wrapping the singles over one another.

When the yarn runs out on one of the two bobbins, your yarn should be ready for completion. If you have breakage on any of the singles, the two broken ends should be slightly overlapped, then continue to ply. The spot will be concealed and secured by the other single.

Once you're done plying, it's now time for your yarn to be taken off of your wheel using a niddy noddy.

Plying With a Drop Spindle

I demonstrated how I spin yarn on a drop spindle in the preceding section on *yarn spinning with a drop spindle (similar to using a spinning wheel)*. Now is the time for your yarn to be plied using a drop spindle and having it prepared for use in a project.

In reality, there are numerous methods for plying on a spindle, including center-pull ball, Andean plying, and multiple spindles. A lazy kate and weaving bobbins can as well be used to hold your singles exactly like you would when plying on a wheel. For our demonstration, we will use the center pull ball method.

Center Pull Ball

Because a spindle used in this demonstration, I'll need to remove the yarn from the spindle. For this, I'll make use of a ball winder in making a center pull ball.

The U-nit ML702 Jumbo ball winder is my preferred ball winder. Yarn can be wound for long with this winder while maintaining a tight tension, so the center pull ball does not fall apart as I ply.

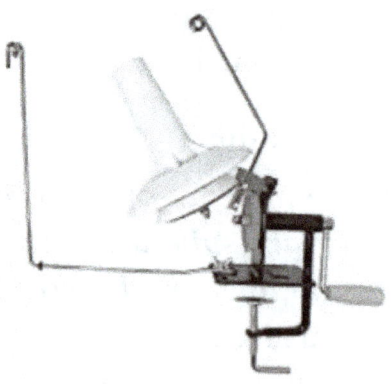

There are many factors to keep in mind while using your center pull ball.

1. When a single is wound into a ball, it retains energy, implying the presence of several twists in it. When putting the single on the ball winder, ensure the tension on it is maintained; else, the yarn will become floppy with curly pigtails forming on it. It has the potential to produce a tangled mess.

2. When the yarn is taken off the ball winder, make sure the ends are aligned. I lay both yarn cake ends side by side so that the twists could wind around one another before I removed them from the winder. They won't unravel or untwist as a result of this. This is the beginning of the twist, which I'll attach to the drop spindle's leader.

Before withdrawing the ball from the winder, hold the ends together so they don't untwist.

3. The center pull ball can vary the twist of the yarn when you ply, depending on how the yarn falls apart from the center pull ball. The twist on one strand of yarn will be greater than the twist on the other. This isn't necessarily a bad thing, but it's something to keep in mind when you want to plan for projects. If you have just a spindle or bobbin, it becomes more convenient to ply using a center pull ball.

Attach to the Leader

I'll fold the leader over by putting the yarn's two ends via the loop at the leader's end. That provides enough grip to get it going without unraveling.

For the yarn to be attached to the leader, fold it back on itself

Spinning Direction

I was turning the spindle in a Z twist orientation when the single of this yarn was spun. The yarn needs to be plied in the reverse direction; else, it will unravel. Plying the yarn in an S twist direction is required (we discussed the Z and S twist in the previous section, kindly revisit that section if you need more clarification)

Add Twist

When you've decided which way to ply, add a twist to the spindle, park it like you did when spinning the single strand of yarn in the previous section, and allow the twist to gravitate into the two strands as they wind off the center pull ball. Additional twists can be added to the spindle once the twist gravitates into the yarn until you can't reach your yarn's length. The yarn should now be wound onto the spindle and have the process repeated till the yarn cake is completely plied.

Tip: Plying is a great avenue to get better in allowing the spindle to drop and dangle while spinning around as a beginner spinner. It's less likely that your single may break or split apart, causing the spindle to fall out.

When the twist builds up into the yarn, maintain it under tension. The spindle's weight (if it's hanging freely) will provide support in creating tension. Allowing the yarn to ply as it pleases will result in curly pigtails in the final yarn.

If you're utilizing a drop spindle with a top whorl, ensure the cop you make has a tapered shape. Keeping the spindle's center of gravity nearer to the whorl allows it to spin smoothly without becoming unstable.

N.B: The cop is not an integral component of the spindle at first, but it does play a role in the anatomy of the spindle as it develops. A cop or a ball is formed by winding a strand of yarn or thread around the spindle shaft or whorl after it has been spun.

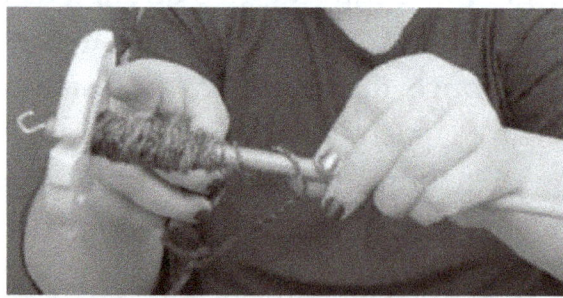

To maintain a well-balanced spin, the yarn should be wound close to the whorl

I highly recommend purchasing or constructing a little niddy noddy once you're done plying, with the yarn ready to be removed from your spindle. My one-yard niddy noddy is ideal for removing projects from spindles and samples from bobbins.

I'll tie the yarn into a skein once I've pulled it from the spindle and get it ready for the finishing phase.

Other Methods of Plying (Navajo or Chain Ply)

My preferred method of plying yarn is Navajo or Chain plying. There are a number of reasons why Navajo (Chain) plying is advantageous for making handspun, and we'll go over them shortly.

Plying Yarn With Navajo (Chain) Method

Navajo plying is a fantastic option if you have just one handspun yarn bobbin that you'd like to ply. It will take some time to master, and you should go gradually at first.

To avoid spoiling your handspun yarn, I strongly advise you to first try it with some scrap or commercially produced yarn.

The main idea of Navajo plying is to crochet a large chain and then let all the chain strands (three strands) ply one another.

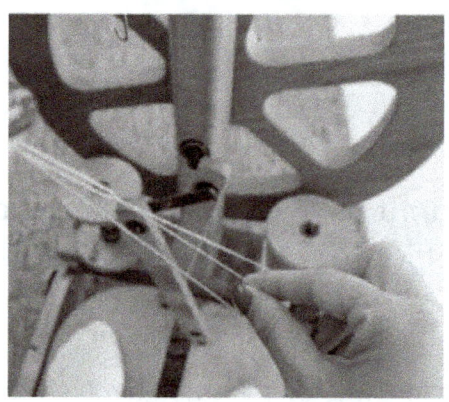

Navajo Plying Is Approproriate For:

Repurposing 2 ply scraps: Because it's practically impossible to precisely have the same length/ quantity of yarn on two single bobbins, you'll invariably end up with a few more on one compared to the other. Chain plying is a great way to use up any leftover yarn.

Maintaining color separation: This method of plying yarn aids in the preservation of dyed fiber color sequences. Imagine a long single bobbin spun from a lovely braid of roving with dyed-in-sections. Instead of making a more multicolored yarn, this single bobbin, when chain plied, will keep the colors separate rather than the more multicolored yarn that a 2 ply would produce. Once you've gotten a little more expertise in chain plying, you can even decide to make the color changes fall at one of your loop's ends.

The first image shown below is a 2 ply yarn (The colors of the two singles mix and play off one another, striking at various spots to create a wonderful effect.), whereas the second image is chain plied.

Steps For Navajo/Chain Ply – With a Spinning Wheel

1. Place the bobbin you'll be plying near one side of your body. (Because I construct my loops with my right hand, I place mine on my right.) You don't want it too far off that you pull so much off the bobbin at once; this could cause it to double back or create a knot. I'm utilizing the peg on my Ashford Kiwi 3 spinning wheel.

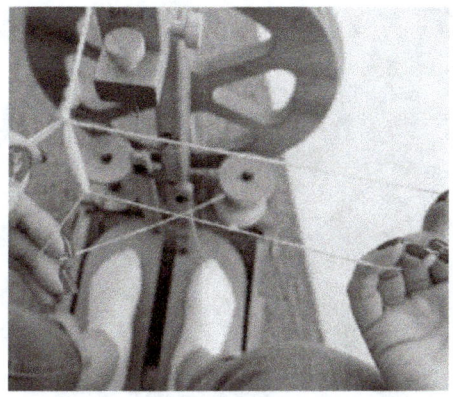

2. Begin by tying your single to a fresh bobbin's leader.

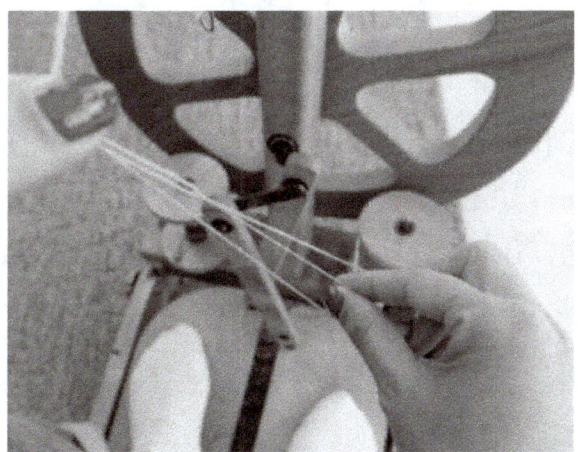

3. Create a loop so you can pull the single through it afterward. (Like a huge crocheted chain.)

4. Grab a segment of the single and construct a large chain by pulling down toward the bobbin (located near your "back" hand).

5. Maneuver the ply with the "front" of your hand (in this case, my left). With your right hand (the other hand) making the loops, ensure that the twist does not go beyond the front hand.

6. Allow the bobbin to feed onto the yarn that was plied.

7. Once you're done plying, it's time for your yarn to be taken off your wheel using a niddy noddy.

Tips For Navajo Plying:

1. The single should always be plied in the reverse direction from how you spun it. If you used a Z twist to spin your single, you'd need to ply it using an S twist. If the single was spun using an S twist, you'd need to ply it with a Z twist.

2. SLOW DOWN! And when I say slow, I mean it. Take your time, even once you've gotten the hang of it.

3. Slowly, pull the single while building your chains/loops, rather than yanking it off the bobbin.

4. Maintain close proximity to the bobbin. Ensure the bobbin is closer to your right knee if you'd be using your right hand to make the loops/chains.

5. Make sure the yarn doesn't double back on itself. Slowing down can help you avoid this.

6. Keep your hands apart as much as possible. If you get your hands too close together, the chain/loop will become very small, causing you to lose control of the twist.

7. As you ply the yarn, keep an eye on it and make sure it's balanced.

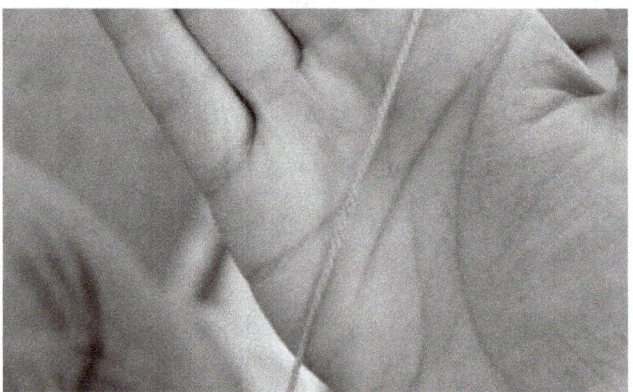

8. Each time the loops/chains connect, there will be little bumps. Although the bumps aren't evident once the yarn is done and set, you can make longer loops for lesser bumps.

9. Navajo/Chain plying very hairy yarns is more difficult since the longer fibers might get stuck between the loops, making it difficult to generate a yarn that's balanced.

Perform test cases of plying with the Navajo/Chain method with some commercially created or scrap yarn before using your own handspun. In the long run, you'll thank yourself.

Steps For Navajo/Chain Ply – With a Drop Spindle

1. Wind your single onto a spare spindle, a bobbin, or anything else that will let you pull it up easily. You may quickly wind the yarn off if there is an extra spindle by holding it between your feet with the shaft pointing up.

2. A loop (slip knot) should be made, similar to when you start a crochet chain.

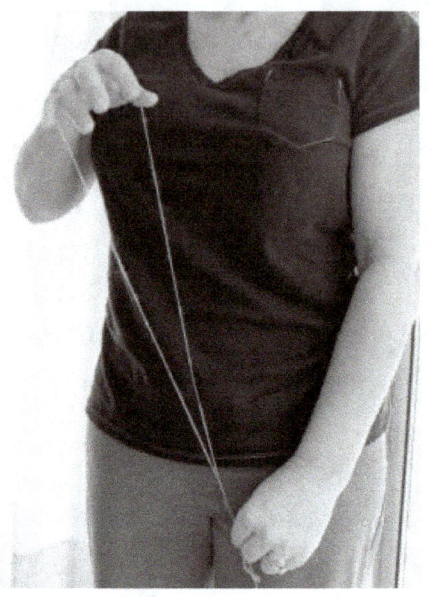

3. Attach the loop's end (the part shown at the base of the image above) to your spindle's hook by winding it down several twists onto the shaft from the whorl, then winding back up over it to secure it.

4. Secure the loop through the hook with your fingers open, then pull the end of the singles to be plied through the loop to make another loop.

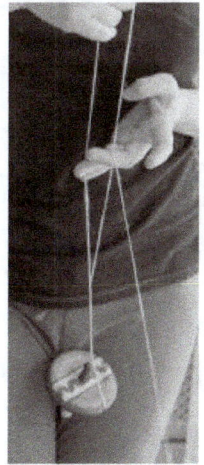

5. Spin in the reverse direction where the singles were first spun and ensure your fingers are used to keep the loop open while you hold the singles' free end to be plied in the same hand. (Apologies for the poor visuals in this photo)

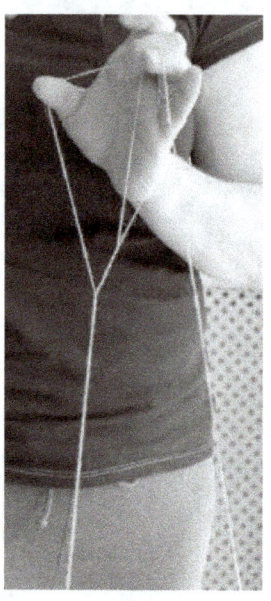

While winding plied yarn onto the spindle, the loop should be kept open.

Try to keep the singles from rubbing against one other when they're looped.

6. Repeat the previous three procedures till the plying is finished. The loop should be kept open if you come to a halt at the center by using any technique deemed fit.

Resolving Yarn Plying Problems

Plied yarns have a consistent texture, are stronger, endure longer, and are less likely to tangle. Here are some frequent questions and challenges you could run into when practicing plying and their solutions.

What should I do if one of my singles breaks or if I've finished one and need to start a new one?

You're bound to damage one of the singles you're plying sooner or later. Make no attempt to tie a knot. Knots always leave an ugly bulge in the yarn as well as a weak area. Make a splice instead by doing the following: Spread the two singles apart, insert the fresh thread between them, turn the wheel, and let the twist bond the singles together.

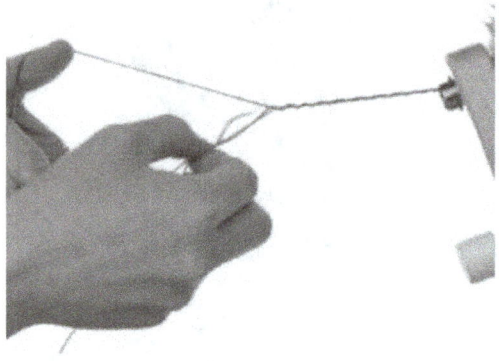

You could use the same method if you've reached the single's end on one bobbin and need to add another. This would create a small section where the three singles are grouped together, but this should go unnoticed.

I'm unsure how much ply twist I'll require

Plying singles is one way of making a balanced yarn. When knit or woven, a balanced yarn hangs straight and lies evenly throughout the cloth.

Before you begin plying, double-check the twist in your single. Make a balanced ply with a hook to see how it looks and feels. Grasp the twist with your fingertips. If you enjoy the way it looks and feels, you should try plying with a similar twist. To confirm that your twisted yarn and plied yarn are similar, count how many twists it has per inch and measure it.

Sometimes the yarn isn't what you are actually looking for. You can alter it by introducing more twists to the single (spin it again to the right) or subtracting some twists (run it to the left via the wheel). A plied yarn's balance is controlled by the single.

Which whorl should I use when plying on a wheel?

Several spinning wheels come with two-groove whorls. Traditional spinners spin woolen in the larger groove and ply woolen in the smaller groove. For worsted, they do the opposite, spinning on the small groove and plying on the larger.

My plying is uneven

Count your foot beats as you spin if your skein appears to have several areas of inconsistent plying. This classic spinning procedure ensures that each length you bring out has the same amount of ply twist. As you begin to enter the ply twist, count each time you treadle. You should just keep treadling if you arrive at the fiber hand before you have the same number of twists as the last draw. Feed the yarn into the wheel as rapidly as possible, using half the number of treadles you used to draw it out.

Tip: This also fixes the problem of a skein with a loosely plied beginning and a tightly plied end. This issue arises because an empty bobbin pulls the yarn ahead faster than a full bobbin. Counting sees that the twist is equally distributed in the yarn before you wind the yarn onto the bobbin.

The woolen I'm plying is constantly breaking

If the woolen you're plying is continuously breaking, especially if you're using really fine, short fibers like cashmere or yak, let it sit on the bobbin for a day or two before plying. It should be a lot more stable now.

My plied yarn has loops with texture and curled edges

The plied yarn might sometimes appear to have a curled edge or even little loops. This occurs when the singles' tension is uneven; if one single is looser, it wraps around the tighter one. To resolve this issue, figure out which single is loose and adjust your fingers to apply a bit extra pressure to it.

Finishing Handspun Yarn

You've done it; your handspun yarn has been wound onto a bobbin or spun on a spindle. But "it ain't done unless it's done." Newly spun yarn needs to be washed or steamed to set the twist, just like a knitted or freshly sewn clothing that isn't finished until it's been washed and blocked. Some spinners prefer working with yarns that have been newly spun (for example, those who prefer "energized" yarns with active twist or those who plan weaving with their handspun, finishing it as cloth); however, several knitters will discover that yarns act properly and more predictably if some extra steps are taken before using their handspun. So, review the steps in finishing your handspun yarn.

Winding a Skein

Before your yarn is washed or steamed, a skein must first be made. Spinners with a complete arsenal of tools can wind a skein using a niddy-noddy or reel and using a lazy kate to put a complete bobbin on it, but those just getting started can improvise. A shoebox can be used to accommodate your bobbin or spindle while your yarn is wound off between your elbow and hand.

A niddy-noddy or reel is a great investment for people that spins constantly. It's easier to demonstrate than to describe how to utilize a niddy-noddy.

Maintain even tension (do not pull overly hard) and move in one direction.

Niddy-noddies help you wind a skein that is longer than your arm can hold, and reels [see below] are much more effective as they rise up by themselves, allowing you wind yarn much faster.

Winding skeins into 2 or 1 1/2-yard skeins (if you're not sure what size of skein is produced by your niddy-noddy or reel, you can wind some leftover yarn once over it and take your measurement) is common with niddy-noddies and reels. Then the number of strands on one of the skein's sides should be counted and multiplied by the skein's length to estimate the number of yards available.

If you utilized an alternative (such as your arm), you'd need to deduce your yardage by measuring the length of a complete wrap. I get lucky occasionally when the final piece of yarn gets to the start of the skein as I wind it, but in most cases, I'd have to close any opening using scrap yarn.

After all the yarn from your bobbin or spindle has been wound off, tie the skein in 3 to 5 places with a figure-8 knot to ensure it doesn't get tangled while washing or dyeing it. I like to make my ties out of some crochet cotton made of white color since it's easy to locate and cut off when it is time.

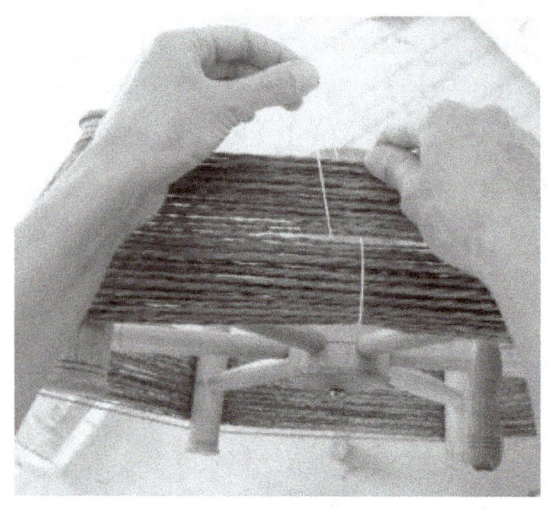

Washing or Steaming

To set yarn's twist is to "finish" your yarn, as it is commonly called. The twist in your yarn can be set when you wash or steam it.

Use a chopstick or tongs in holding your yarn while steaming it, or put it on the niddy-noddy while calmly passing it across the steam that comes from a teakettle. A garment steamer can also be used as a replacement if there is any available. Put on an oven mitt and keep an eye on your body parts because steam burns! Wait for some minutes of drying time before using the yarn. It's important to remember that when you steam a yarn on a niddy-noddy, it is the same as drying under tension;

there could be variations in your gauge after the yarn is washed, so it is better to wash with a swatch first. While steaming is faster, I prefer washing my skeins after spinning to ensure they are clean and fit for knitting.

Everyone appears to have their unique washing routine for their woolies, but here's what I do. Wool and other animal fibers should be soaked for 10 minutes (at least) in warm to hot soapy water before being washed clean. Dish soap, no-rinse wool wash, or shampoo can be used. To avoid mistakenly felting the fibers, don't agitate or wring. Even though garment labels advise that sweaters be washed only in cold water, I wash several of my completed skeins in hot water. I like removing any leftover oils or too much dye with hot water, and I prefer shrinking anything that may shrink first before I start knitting; I've never had an issue with felting.

Plant fibers like linen and cotton are best completed when you use dish detergent to boil the skeins in a pot filled with water and on the stove for 40 min. (at least). To dye yarn made of cotton, you will have to soak it in water with detergent and two teaspoons of soda ash (known also as washing soda) to eliminate the natural waxes that may impede even color absorption. My linen and cotton yarns are boiled in skein form (tied in numerous places to avoid tangling) because I knit with them; those who finish linen or cotton singles for weaving can choose plastic cores to boil them on.

Your clean skein should be taken out from the rinse water to finish the washing or steaming phase and then squeezed mildly to drain the surplus water and laid flat on a towel. Roll up the towel and squeeze out as much liquid as possible.

The next step, thwacking or sometimes called snapping, appears to be a personal preference, and doing it or not depends on the fibers you've used (it's best to avoid doing this with fragile fibers). Thwacking provides your

141

skein a little shock, which helps to further secure your fibers in place and fluff things up. To thwack, you simply smack your moist skein against a smooth, hard surface. (it's best to do it outside or in a spot that's easy to clean; it'll splash water!) You can also snap your yarn a half-dozen times like a whip. Here, my skein was taken in one end and beaten against the bathtub's side after eliminating all extra water. Then I took the opposite end and thwacked it as well. This allowed the fibers to settle even deeper into one other, giving my yarn a fuzzy appearance.

When you are done with the above, allow your yarn to hang from your hand to see how well it is balanced. The yarn is balanced if it does not twist on itself (or at least not too much). However, if there are still a lot of twists, then all is not lost.

Drying

Finally, we'll dry our final yarn by hanging it out to dry. If it's raining, this can be done in the shower or outside on the fence, clothesline, or other suitable location. If your yarn still has that extra twist, you can add some weight to the loop's bottom (such as a spray bottle) to pull the fibers into shape.

My yarn is hung to dry in the absence of tension since my handspun is used to knit while keeping any native elasticity.

Twisting the Skein

You may twist your skein into a neat small storage package after it's dry. Twist a side of the skein that's open in a particular direction till there is a twist on the skein back on itself while holding the skein that's open at every loop's end.

You may either turn the yarn into a hank by slipping the loop's ends into each other or winding it into a ball once it has dried.

There you have it: you have finished your yarn, and it's now time for crocheting, weaving, or knitting.

A Short message from the Author:

Hey, I hope you are enjoying the book? I would love to hear your thoughts!

Many readers do not know how hard reviews are to come by and how much they help an author.

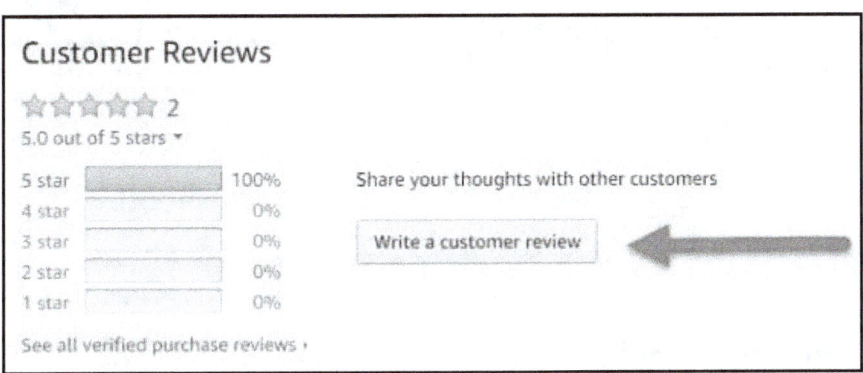

I would be incredibly grateful if you could take just 60 seconds to write a short review on Amazon, even if it is a few sentences!

>> Click here to leave a quick review

Thanks for the time taken to share your thoughts!

Chapter 4

Troubleshooting Yarn Spinning Problems

When you first start to spin, things can and, I'm sad to say, almost always go wrong. Your yarn will either not wind on at all or will wind on too tightly. Alternatively, you may find yourself helplessly asking, "Where did the end go?!

Don't be discouraged no matter what happens! With some spinning-wheel and spindle troubleshooting, we hope to alleviate your frustration.

Spinning Wheel Problems

The wheel glides across the floor when I put my foot down

If you are spinning to the right, ensure the footman is at 1 o'clock before pushing down on the treadle. Ensure the footman is at 11 o'clock if spinning to the left. If the footman is treadled at 12 o'clock, there will be a jam in the wheel that will force you to push it over the floor.

Beginner spinners frequently believe that the floor's surface is too polished, leading the wheel to slip off.

If the scotch brake is tightened sufficiently for my yarn to pull on, the wheel will not turn

Allow a small amount of brake band tension to be released. When the wheel revolves as it should, and the yarn is pulling in appropriately, the problem will be solved. A turning wheel without the yarn pulling in at the desired speed, means you should loosen the drive band's tension just enough for the yarn to pull in at the desired speed.

The yarn gets tangled between the flyer and the bobbin all the time

This occurs as a result of uneven treadling. Simply disconnect it, reconnect it, and begin again. Also, the bobbin could have been overly full, which will cause the yarn to pour over the bobbin's edge and twist around the shaft.

I have to cling to the yarn with both hands

If it's a single-drive wheel, some of the brake band's tension should be relaxed; if it's a double-drive wheel, try to reduce the tension on both bands. Make sure it's on a medium-sized whorl; a whorl that's too big will cause the yarn to pull in too quickly.

I have the impression that I am squeezing the yarn into the wheel

If you're using a single-drive wheel, the scotch brake's tension should be tightened, or the flyer and bobbin if a double-drive wheel is used.

Pay attention to the whorl you're on; if it's too little, the yarn will be twisted a lot.

A high-twist yarn's resistance (tension) can sometimes be enough to ensure the wheel does not pull it onto the bobbin. In this situation, it should be broken off and started all over.

Ensure your bobbin isn't completely filled; this will make it difficult to add more yarn. Also, ensure no hook has trapped the yarn with nothing preventing it from feeding onto the wheel.

Finally, ensure the bobbin on the flyer is working smoothly. When the humidity changes, it can also cause the bobbins to swell.

My yarn appears to have a good twist but continues to break while pulling it back

Did you leave the break on? If you did, this would exert so much pressure, forcing the yarn to break when delicate yarn from a bobbin is pulled.

The bobbin can be filled halfway, but it won't feed any more yarn after that

The more the bobbin is full, the nearer it is in size to the flyer, and the lesser the yarn's pull. As the bobbin is filling up, slightly tighten the brake's tension or the double-drive band tension to continuously maintain the wheel's pull on the yarn.

Why Won't My Yarn Wind On?

When you're first starting out, this is one of the most typical spinning-wheel issues. Check sure everything on the wheel is in its proper location first. Is your drive band properly seated? Is your bobbin in the right place? Is your braking system activated?

The twist in the yarn causes it to loop back on itself and get trapped all the time. The problem may be due to insufficient brake tension. Remove the brake band and reinstall it with the tension set very loosely. Gradually raise the tension until you can feel the yarn pulled into the orifice by the wheel. You want as much tension to pull the yarn in without yanking it out of your hands.

It's conceivable that you're holding the yarn too firmly and it's not winding on. Beginners frequently grasp the fiber supply with both hands, but you must let go a little to allow the spun yarn to wound on.

My Yarn Winds On So Tightly!

The brake tension is excessively tight if you feel like you're struggling with the wheel as though it will tear the spun and not-yet-spun fiber from your hands.

Remove the brake band and reinstall it with very loose tension. Gradually raise the tension until you feel the yarn being pulled into the orifice by the wheel. Try to also put your drive band on a large enough whorl, which will slow down the twisting of the fiber.

My Wheel Always Goes Backwards!

You need to work on your technique. To ensure it constantly goes in one way, then the other, try to treadle with no fiber on the wheel. Ensure to remember the intended position of the drive wheel with regard to the treadles for it to revolve in the desired direction. It's also quite OK for the wheel to be steered in the correct direction with your hand.

Treadling is So Hard!

Examine your wheel to ensure that all drive band tension and hooks are in good working order.

Adding some spinning-wheel oil drops to the working elements of your spinning wheel will assist in lubricating and minimizing friction. Treadling typically needs additional force on bobbin-led wheels with Irish tension, such as some Louet spinning wheels.

The Bobbin Has Blobs of Yarn!

Change the hooks or the slide clip more frequently. Because you're close to the bobbin's core while you're just getting started on a new bobbin, you will need to replace hooks frequently. Winding on at a bobbin's end, then working your way up a hook at a time to the bobbin's other end before you return is usually a great idea.

The WooLee Winder is a wonderful option if you'd rather spin instead of changing hooks. This flyer is designed to accommodate various spinning wheels, and it employs gears to move the yarn guide in an up and down fashion along the bobbin while spinning.

I Can't Find The End of My Yarn!

Stop spinning and examine your bobbin carefully. If you massage it a bit more, the yarn end might pop out. Take a look around that area to figure out the hook you were on. You may also check to ascertain if something comes loose by running a transparent tape along (up and down) the bobbin.

If you still cannot locate the end, a last-ditch alternative is to cut a strand of singles around the area you feel you've lost it, pulling the yarn away from the bobbin until the end shows up.

Drop Spindle Problems

Fibers separate or won't stay together AFTER I spin them

This indicates that there is no sufficient twist in your fibers to keep them together. As the fiber is fed into the twist, ensure the motion of the spin is not being stalled or interrupted by your fingers; occasionally, when your fingers are pulled away, the string gets plucked, causing your spindle to slow down. Examine the single you have spun: if the twist's angle is compared to a clock, set it anywhere between 1 and 2 (or 10 and 11; that's if you're spinning in a counterclockwise fashion).

Also, be sure you're not eliminating twists while winding the single onto your spindle's shaft. Twist can be added or removed with an overhand motion, so double-check the style you adopted there. Thin singles also require more twists than thick ones.

Fibers drift away or won't stay together AS they are spun

This means no twist is not penetrating the fibers before the spindle's weight pushes them apart. Your fiber hand should firmly be supporting the fibers until the fibers pass across the drafting zone and enters the twist.

Also, per the fiber you are working with, the quantity of twist you'll require varies. For example, merino fibers require less twists than alpaca fibers to keep them together, and fibers that are short require more twists than fibers that are long.

Single kinks up in places

This could indicate a couple of problems, including too many twists and your single having thick and thin areas. Twists gravitate from areas that are thick toward thin areas, making the thick areas appear underspun while the tiny spots keep twisting back on themselves. It merely takes experience to spin a uniform single, and having your source of fiber supply loosened but managed can also help.

Yarns that are overspun will seem overspun throughout the single's length. Small pigtails and hard patches will appear, and your single might also break apart from thin areas.

Pigtails: way too much twist!

If it's only some yards overspun, your spindle can be locked and have the single unrolled for some yards while drafting more unspun fiber from your source of fiber to provide somewhere for your extra twist to go to. Better still, you can simply unspin your spindle till the pigtails disappear. If most of your single has been overspun, ensure the spindle is locked in while using another spindle to gradually spin in the reverse direction to remove a few of the extra twists.

I want my single to be fine /thick

It all comes down to the quantity of fiber you release at a given time into the twist. Less fiber equals a finer single, while more fiber equals a thicker single. It's not always easy to figure out the quantity of fiber needed, but it's usually lesser than you imagine. Dismantle a yarn that you wish to mimic that is composed of fiber comparable to what you are spinning to figure out the quantity needed: singles should be broken up, then untwisted and the number of fibers twisted in it should be counted. Then, using a little amount of fiber, practice drafting a similar amount. Note that the amount of twist required varies depending on what your single's diameter is: thicker singles require less twist, while finer singles require more.

156

My single has thick and thin spots

Uneven drafting is frequently the cause. Normally, the recommendation before spinning is for your fibers to be loosened to enable them to pull effortlessly via your hands and into the twist. On the other hand, you must be cautious when you want to pre-draft your fiber: if you draw so hard, your source of fiber could have thick and thin spots that may cause your single to also have thick and thin spots. If you're pre-drafting, pull till the initial 'give' is felt.

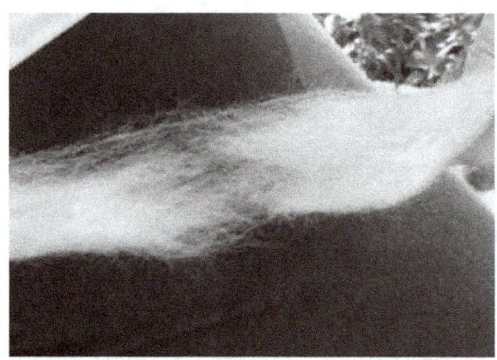

Pre-drafting can help create a thin spot in your single.

Conversely, you can free up the fibers in a braid by carefully spreading them out throughout the width rather than the braid's length.

My spindle ceases to spin correctly and begins unspinning when it shouldn't

This is likely an indication that your spindle is too light for the thickness of the single you are spinning. Before pausing and unspinning, your spindle should spin for many seconds. Try spinning a single that's thin to test. If it addresses the issue, you can upgrade your spindle to a heavier one to achieve your desired thicker single.

The single constantly breaks away at the join when a fresh fiber is added

This happens for one of three reasons: the fibers were not overlapped enough, they were not allowed to 'mesh' together sufficiently, or a very thick single at the join with the twist jumping across it to the thin spots. There should be an overlapping of fibers in a join for at least 1 to 2″ or more if the fibers are slippery or short, and less if the fibers are 'grabbier' and longer. It's also crucial to splay out the joining fibers' ends so they may latch on and interlock together more easily. Finally, let the joining fibers diminish in thickness into the single's end; if the two ends have the same thickness as the single, you'll have a spot that's thick, making the twist spread around instead of in the join.

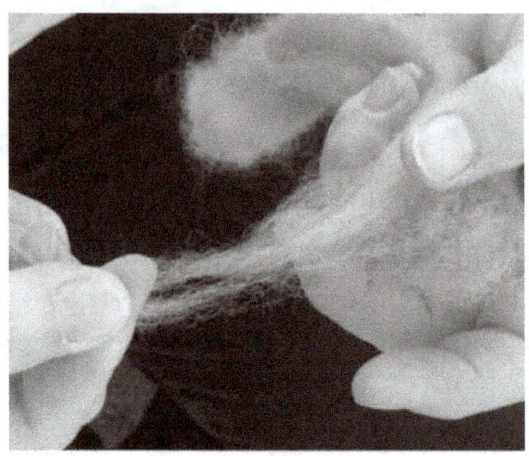

Overlap splayed-out fibers at least 1-2 inches to make a strong join.

While I'm spinning, my single breaks

The cause can be either of two things;

- When you overspin, which then places excess tension on a spot that's thin

- When the spindle you are using to spin is very heavy for the single being made.

Examine your single for spots that are both thin and thick; as you learn the art of spinning consistent singles, the presence of thin and thick spots will cause the breakage to reduce. Try switching to a less heavy (lighter) spindle as well; you might find that doing so will help you avoid overspinning.

My single breaks while I'm plying

Check to see if your singles can smoothly unwind from the ball or bobbins on which they were wound on. You will want a good amount of tension to ensure your singles do not get tangled; however, ensure they don't have too much tension.

Also, you're probably plying with a heavier spindle. Examine the yarn you plied to see if one single is swirling over the other and the other is virtually straight.

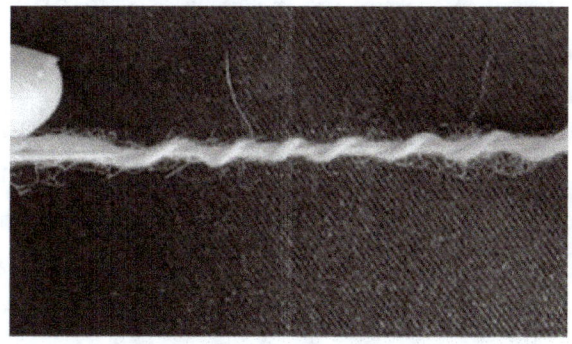

Uneven tension when plying puts strain on the straight single

If this is the case, the tension between the singles is uneven, implying that the straight single is bearing the spindle's weight. If it's both thick and thin, you'll need to be particularly cautious. Adjust the hold you have on the singles for them to feed into the twist of the ply with consistent tension, and if possible, decrease the yarn lengths you are plying before you wind it onto the spindle.

In most cases, my spindle wobbles while spinning

Practice spindle spinning without the yarn being spun by tying a finished length of yarn to the hook. Practice creating a smooth 'snap' without allowing the spindle to swing. Try a very smooth spin while at it to examine the alignment between the hook and yarn across the shaft of the spindle. If there's an out-of-place hook that is bent, the yarn won't center correctly along with the shaft's direction, which might cause a wobble.

Additionally, as the spun fiber is wound onto the spindle's shaft, experiment with placing the cop in several locations on the spindle, starting with winding the single immediately beneath the whorl. The cop's weight influences the way the spindle spins as it acquires more spun fiber. Also, experiment with other cop shapes, such as a ball versus a 'hive' shape.

The end… almost!

Hey! We've made it to the final chapter of this book, and I hope you've enjoyed it so far.

If you have not done so yet, I would be incredibly thankful if you could take just a minute to leave a quick review on Amazon

Reviews are not easy to come by, and as an independent author with a little marketing budget, I rely on you, my readers, to leave a short review on Amazon.

Even if it is just a sentence or two!

So if you really enjoyed this book, please...

>> Click here to leave a brief review on Amazon.

I truly appreciate your effort to leave your review, as it truly makes a huge difference.

Chapter 5

Maintaining The Spinning Wheel

A spinning wheel is a significant investment, and you want to get it going as smoothly as possible. What exactly does that imply? Maintenance is required on a regular basis. It's not difficult; simply oil, clean, and nourish the wood. Your wheel will appreciate it.

Tip #1: Make Sure It's Well Oiled

Any point of friction on your spinning wheel requires oil. The majority of spinners utilize commercial oil supplied by the wheel's manufacturer.

Some spinners choose natural products such as olive oil or vegetable oil, perhaps blended with a drop of aromatic essential oil such as lavender, lemon, or rose. In general, liquid oil is the most effective. (Vaseline becomes gummy.) Sewing machine oil and silicone fishing-reel oil are also effective. Dab a little oil on a towel and gently wipe the various parts that needs oiling.

Common places for oiling your wheel include:

1. The area around the bobbin where movement occurs (not where the yarn touches; you don't want oily yarn).
2. The area around the flyer where movement occurs (again, not where the yarn touches).
3. The area around the wheel where movement occurs (where the treadles attach to the wheel).
4. The area on the treadles where movement occurs (where the treadles attach to the wheel frame)
5. The wheel's axle
6. The leather connector between the treadle and the footman.
7. The crank bearings and rods
8. All other components that move

How Often Should The Wheel Be Oiled?

Some spinners advocate oiling the wheels after every 8 hours of use. Others just oil their wheels when there is squeaking. If you spin most times, it's a good idea to oil once a month, or once every season if you don't. After each outdoor event, oil it to remove debris from the crevices.

Tip #2: Keep the Wood Clean

It's easy to get filthy when on-the-go with your wheel. The wood will get dirty even if you spin yarn outside. Lemon essential oil can be used as a natural cleanser. Simply dab a little on a towel and gently wipe the wood.

Orange Glo (several spinners shy away from applying any silicone-based product on the wood) or Old English Lemon Oil are two commercial products that perform nicely.

Tip #3: Nourish The Wood and Protect It

Different spinners choose different spinning wheel finishes. Some spinners opt for a painted appearance. If you want to maintain things as natural as possible, here's how to preserve the finish:

- To keep the wood moist (especially if it is an unfinished wheel), use a wood wax or preserver. Olive oil, beeswax, and essential oil are used to make them. The wax "seals" the wood while the preserver is soaked into it. Repeat the application process every 6 months or as required.

166

- Try all-natural Blue Mountain Handcrafts Wood Balm if you want a less greasy, matte finish product. Repeat the application process every six months or as required.

- Paste Wax Floor Polish, Butchers Wax (for butcher block tables), and Feed-n-Wax Polish are commercially available products.

- Silicone-based products (such as Pledge) are not advised since they cause the wood to be excessively slippery, making the drive band to hop.

Tip #4: Replace Maintenance Parts and Keep Out of Sunlight

The flyer's hooks may need to be replaced occasionally as well. Some wheel manufacturers may provide flyer hooks, leather or plastic treadle connectors, drive band, and oil in a maintenance pack.

Keep your wheel out of direct sunlight, away from heat, and in a humid atmosphere. If you do, your wheel may warp, and you will need to have it repaired by a

167

professional. It's also possible that you'll have to replace everything.

Conclusion

Wow!

We've reached the conclusion of this excellent read. If you've made it this far in this book, I congratulate you; you're the type of person who succeeds.

Yarn spinning is an amazing craft for anyone who loves the idea of spinning their own fiber to produce a customizable yarn that they can use to knit or crochet a certain kind of project. The flexibility of being able to spin your own yarn to achieve your desired objective is so fulfilling, and that's just one of the beauties associated with yarm spinning. Yarn spinning is also therapeutic and highly addictive, which could cause you to neglect your everyday activities. As a result, you must thread with caution. Keep in mind not to get drawn in. Set aside time for other important pursuits, so be warned!.

Ensure to absorb every information shared in this book on the processes and techniques of spinning your own yarn, the tools and supplies needed, and how to get the right tools and supplies to work with.

169

As with any new skills you learn (even for skills already learned, mistakes are bound to happen), you won't become an expert in a day. Prepare to make numerous mistakes but, most importantly, learn from them. Allowing your mistakes to hold you back will only keep you from forging ahead. If you keep going, you'll reach a point where you won't make many mistakes (even experts still make mistakes). I have taken out time to educate you on several of the mistakes spinners typically encounter, so ensure you go over them repeatedly and refer to them when you make any mistake and get stuck in between.

So, grab the bull by the horn and start spinning those beautiful yarns today.

Don't be scared!

Relax and take it easy on yourself!

You've got this, spinner!

www.ingramcontent.com/pod-product-compliance
Lightning Source LLC
Chambersburg PA
CBHW071148120626
46546CB00006B/2168